When God puts His creative glory inside you, it gives you the courage to invent, experiment, grow, take risks, break rules, make mistakes, and have fun! That's why I'm so excited about this new book, *Creative Glory*, by my friend Joshua Mills. As you read this book, your creativity will be awakened and activated in a new way!

—*Rick Pino*
Founder, Heart of David Movement, Austin, TX
www.worshipcoach.com

I know of no one better to release this message than my friend Joshua Mills. Joshua is an authority on the subject of creative glory, as he is a gifted artist, an anointed songwriter, and a prolific author. Joshua flows in all manner of creative expression from heaven, and it is my honor to recommend his latest book to you. *Creative Glory* will inspire you to reach out in faith to experience God's creative flow, which will manifest itself through the natural and supernatural DNA God has gifted you with. As you take your place alongside those in Scripture who have done the same, you will release kingdom creativity to solve the "unsolvable." With increased faith, you will look to Jesus, tune to His river of glory, and release His abundance in you and through you to others. It's all part of God's gift of salvation. Experience a greater revelation of the Creator's nature through you today!

—*Dr. Mark Virkler*
Cofounder, Communion with God Ministries
President, Christian Leadership University
Author of numerous books, including *Overflow of the Spirit* and
4 Keys to Hearing God's Voice

Our God is Creator—and He hasn't stopped creating. God inspires creativity—creative glory—in and through His people. Joshua Mills has given us prophetic insight into God as Creator and how His creative glory is available to every believer. The practical lessons with scriptural backing in this innovative book will awaken you to new realms of creative ideas, creative power, creative provision, and, yes, creative glory. This book, in itself, is a manifestation of creative glory. It will shift your mind and shift your life!

—*Jennifer LeClaire*
Founder, Awakening House of Prayer Global Movement
Best-selling author, *Breaking the Miracle Barrier*

Many of us are living in the darkest season of our lifetimes—but there is always hope in God. In his book *Creative Glory*, Joshua Mills gives us insight and inspiration for how to increase our joy, our wisdom, and—more important—the presence of God's glory in our lives through the power of the Holy Spirit. This isn't just a book you will love to read. It's a book you *need* to read to navigate today's challenges.

—*Bishop Clint Brown*
Judah Church, Orlando, FL
Singer, songwriter, and international speaker

When Joshua Mills speaks of creative glory, there is nothing theoretical about it. He practices it every day and has done so for many years. I have been a witness of this over the past few years as I have worked with him on his best-selling books. Twenty-five and thirty years ago, when I sat with the late Ruth Ward Heflin and helped her put together her now-famous glory series of books, she would occasionally reach up (physically) into the glory realm and pull down an answer she was looking for, or sometimes the answer would come to her with the touch of angel wings. Joshua mines that same heavenly realm, and the results bless us all.

—*Harold McDougal*
Author and editor
Owner, McDougal & Associates

Joshua Mills has done it again! He has managed to pull out yet another revelation of the glory dimension, and this one really got me fired up. The creative-glory realm opens up divine intelligence and ideas to help you surge ahead. We need to live in that kind of glory, and *Creative Glory* serves as a heavenly road map.

—*Ryan LeStrange*
Author, *Breaking Curses*
Founder, Ryan LeStrange Ministries and ATL Hub

Joshua Mills has given his life to discovering where human creativity and the glory of God intersect. We are living in an hour when God's glory is breaking through the realm of the invisible to the realm of the visible through all expressions of creativity. *Creative Glory* is an awakening cry to those who will bring heaven to earth through Holy Spirit-inspired ingenuity. This book will guide you in your own pursuit to discover the God of all creativity and His *Creative Glory*.

—*Jeff and Suzanne Whatley*
Worship leaders and recording artists
King's Way Music, Birmingham, AL

Creative Glory is not just packed with information but also contains revelation that will bring transformation. As I read these much-needed and timely truths from Joshua Mills, I could literally feel the glory realm invade my thoughts and my environment. I believe that this book will open new vistas in the Spirit to you that will release Holy Spirit innovation that is beyond your wildest expectations. I highly recommend this book to propel you into the realm of divine inspiration that will impact not only your life, but also your legacy!

—*Roma Waterman*
Award-winning songwriter, worship leader, and author
Founder, HeartSong Creative Academy and HeartSong Prophetic Alliance

Creative Glory is a blueprint for instant creative inspiration that will ignite your spirit to believe for the extraordinary. Joshua explains how God's Spirit of creativity will literally unlock your goals and dreams as you take a step of faith toward the unknown. Start living a life of success with no limitations.

—*Jack Shocklee*
Shae Shoc Records
beckahshae.com

Finally—a book that speaks to the genius of God and the incredible supernatural power working in creatives! This book will spark that creativity and take it to a whole new level. In *Creative Glory*, Joshua Mills has captured the essence of what releases manifestations of God's glory, and I'm telling you, it will activate you to go deeper in the realm of God!

—*Jenny Weaver*
Worship Pastor, Nations Church, Orlando, FL
www.Jennyweaverworships.com

Best-selling author Joshua Mills has written a must-read for anyone who is ready to connect with creative glory. Read this book and be prepared to dream big dreams. Learn from and become inspired by one of the best creative souls out there!

—*Kim Appelt*
Fashion stylist, TV style expert, and author
www.stylebykimxo.com

Joshua Mills and his ministry have inspired me so much. And Joshua's newest book, *Creative Glory*, is all about inspiration. There are times when every artist—whether a musician, writer, or painter—experiences "creative block." Their ideas just stop flowing, or they struggle to produce something that expresses exactly what they are feeling or thinking. Creative blocks also happen to us in life—sometimes lasting for a *long* time. We don't know what step to take next or how to move forward with the ideas and dreams God has placed inside us. In *Creative Glory*, Joshua shows us how to fully receive from the Father of inspiration and creativity to address every need in our lives, and how to give back to others through the distinct gifts He has given us. Ultimately, God's creative glory flows from His *love*—that surprising, "wild" love that forgives us for our failings, heals our pain, gives us new hope, points us in the right direction, expands our creative abilities, and gives us a brand-new life.

—*Brian "Head" Welch*
Cofounder, Grammy Award-winning band Korn
New York Times best-selling author, *Save Me from Myself*
Costar, Showtime documentary *Loud Krazy Love*

Wow! I love Joshua Mills's book *Creative Glory*! For decades, Joshua has been a pioneering minister with regard to preaching, teaching, writing about, and demonstrating God's glory on earth, but this new book, more than any other, demystifies and explains in great detail the many benefits of God's creative glory. You will find it to be both revelatory in its explanations of the divine functions of God's glory and full of practical advice so that you can best benefit from discovering those blessings. I suggest you read this book several times to get every good thing God wants you to experience.

—*Joan Hunter*
Author and evangelist

Joshua Mills's new book *Creative Glory* is masterfully written to help you be released into your unlimited, outside-the-box, creative adventure with God. Joshua teaches us truth from God's Word, and, through personal testimonies, he encourages us to live a life that merges and collaborates with God's glory. When we experience God's creativity, our thoughts, inspiration, wisdom, and direction flow for every situation. This book is for everyone. Come and experience the joy and excitement of living in God's creative glory.

—*Dustine Kinsella*
Artist, ordained minister, and certified mental health coach

Joshua Mills's book *Creative Glory* is an exciting and timely biblical road map to realizing God's divine and creative purpose for your life...through intentional prayer and time alone with God in His glory realm.

—*Tabitha Fair*
Songwriter and recording artist
Nashville, TN

Joshua Mills is a true gift from God, and he is a blessing to my wife, Destanie, and me. Joshua carries God's glory the way God designed us to. Every time I read anything from him, it empowers me and changes my life as if God were speaking directly to me. For us to carry the glory of God in a high degree, we need to know more about the glory and how it is meant to flow in our lives. Joshua's book *Creative Glory* will enable you to reach beyond your natural way of thinking and tap God's glory in you. I believe your true creativity and gifting will flourish as you apply the inspiration and examples he provides. I encourage you to read this book and allow it to change your life and the lives of others around you.

—*Branden Brim*
His Name Ministries

Joshua Mills's new release, *Creative Glory*, is a timely word for the church, as it contains the eternal truth of God's glory. This book will bring the reader into the revelatory insight necessary to access the creative genius that is in God's mind. There are higher ways and higher thoughts in the glory realm. There are heavenly solutions to all the issues we currently face in society, and there is a personal blueprint for our lives, unveiled by God, when we get caught up in creative glory. My wife and I have been personally blessed by the ministry of Joshua and Janet Mills over the years, and I know there is a tangible impartation for those who will read and take in the truth from this glory-infused book.

—*Charlie Shamp*
Cofounder and President, Destiny Encounters International
Vice President, Renaissance Coalition
Author, *Angels* and *Transfigured*

The keyboard releases the sound of minor chords, and the worship leader gives a soft hum or quietly sings in the Spirit—and the spiritual spontaneity is about to draw in willing participants! My friend, that's the skillfulness and sensitivity that Joshua possess in the realm of the open heavens. To create this realm from the sounds of the eternal, you must know the administration and operation of God's Spirit. Joshua's book *Creative Glory* is going to awaken the clogged wells of mediocrity and produce the DNA of sonship! We are sons of our eternal Father. Thank you, Joshua, for bringing that truth to the forefront again in this season. Let *Creative Glory* stir our generations to occupy new territories and take dominion in all spheres of life. I am excited to be equipped to be creative!

—*Dr. Marina McLean*
Keynote speaker, recording artist, songwriter, and award-winning author
www.DrMarinaMcLean.com

Creative Glory is a must-read. For anyone feeling stuck, for anyone feeling lost in the overcast climate of our modern world, for anyone wondering why they're alive at such a time as this—get your hands on this book. For centuries, unbelievers have led the parade of innovation. However, now, in these unprecedented times, the bride of Christ must arise and shine. Page after page, Joshua Mills breaks us out of our traditional boxes as he beckons the church to embrace her creative identity. I'm always impacted by the way Joshua beautifully imparts his own revelation in his writing, and I know anyone who reads this book will be extremely blessed. *Creative Glory* is our portion as believers, and there's never been a better time than now to embrace it.

—*Daniel T. Newton*
Founder and Overseer, Grace Place Ministries
Author, *The Lost Art of Discipleship*

Years ago, the Holy Spirit spoke into my heart, "Those who will be melted in My presence will be radiant in My glory." *Creative Glory* by Joshua Mills will melt you in His presence. As I read this book, at times, I was no longer reading in the normal sense; instead, I was "drinking" with my eyes, and my mind and heart were being flooded with inspiration—the seed of all creativity. Joshua also imparts nuggets of truth that feed the knowledge of the Holy into our minds. One of my favorites is, "Sow...setbacks as seeds in order to receive a harvest of setups." A brilliant insight! God is setting us up to receive gloriously. As Joshua so aptly illustrates, you cannot lose in the glory. I love this book; it is a feast!

—*Deborah Kendrick*
International speaker and missionary
Ashland, VA

Joshua Mills's life and ministry have profoundly and supernaturally impacted my journey with God—from accurately confirming the creative calling and direction over my life to powerfully releasing and activating me into a momentum of freedom, both personally and in a career as a culinary professional in which creativity is essential! I cannot recommend Joshua and his book *Creative Glory* highly enough. As you read this inspiring and life-giving book, allow the Spirit of God to open your horizons afresh and activate you into higher and higher realms of creative glory and a life without limitations. As Joshua would say, do something you've never done before, see something you've never seen before, go somewhere you've never been before—break out! And as you break out from the old into the new, watch God's creativity flow through your life, to the praise of His glorious grace.

—*Stefan Rose*
Head Pastry Chef, Grantley Hall
Online video content creator
Yorkshire, England

Creative Glory will take you out of stress and striving and show you how to do all things from rest, from ease, and from the Spirit. If you are hungry to experience creative miracles, receive divine direction straight from the throne room, and release your unique expression into the world, then this book is for you. Thank you, Joshua Mills, for making the supernatural accessible and continuing to lead the body of Christ into greater realms of God's creative glory!

—*Robia Scott*
Author, *Counterfeit Comforts*
Actress, *Unplanned*

We often think of creativity only in regard to the expression of music, art, and other talents. Joshua Mills has written this powerful book, *Creative Glory*, to help believers see that creativity, from God's perspective, is His gift to influence, change, and shape our lives with His best in a variety of ways. As you read this book, you will learn how to partner with God to manifest His creative glory in every area of your life.

—*Joseph Harris*
Senior Pastor, Love Center Church, Pasadena, MD
"Best Home Cook in America," *All-Star Academy*, Food Network

In the glory, you are invited by the Spirit to experience supernatural realms of creative God-actions, ideas, assignments, and abilities. For years, Joshua Mills has walked with God in the glory and experienced these very things. There are opportunities to create with God waiting for you in the glory realm. In Joshua's book *Creative Glory*, you will discover the keys to unlock this potential—and that makes this book a must-read.

—*Patricia King*
Author, minister, media host, and producer

I love Joshua Mills. His faith is big. His joy is bigger. His depth of reach in the things of God and the glory is massive. In his new book, *Creative Glory*, the title says it all. Joshua lives his life in creative glory, and this book brings every reader along with him right into God's glory realm. The prophets have been saying it's time to peer into the future and see what God is doing, then begin to create and release it on earth. Well, that is exactly what Joshua does in this book, and he makes it look so *easy*. But, wait, it *is* easy! That is, it's easy if you read this book!

—*Julie Meyer*
Author, *30 Days of Praying the Psalms*
Founder, Into The River online worship community
intotheriver.net

It is a great joy and honor to recommend *Creative Glory*, written by our dear friend Joshua Mills. Joshua's inspiring work will help you understand that there is a greater creative atmosphere available to each one of us. We have full access to God's creative glory, and as we step into this inspirational flow of the Holy Spirit, His life, hope, joy, provision, and wisdom can flow into any situation we may be facing. We encourage you to read this book and enter into God's creative glory today! Choose to create with the Creator and let His life manifest through every aspect of who you are.

—*Joe and Bella Garcia*
Speakers, authors, and apostolic and prophetic leaders
Hosts, *Living Your Best Life with Joe & Bella*
Senior Leaders, The River International Church
Hamilton, Ontario, Canada
www.theriverinyou.com

At the heart of the Christian message is God Himself, waiting for His redeemed people to push into a conscious awareness of the glory of His presence and to engage with open heart His majestic Personhood. In Jeremiah 31:3, God says, "Yes, I have loved you with an everlasting love; therefore, with lovingkindness I have drawn you" (NKJV). And Colossians 1:16 states, "For by Him all things were created that are in heaven and that are on earth, visible and invisible, whether thrones or dominions or principalities or powers. All things were created through Him and for Him" (NKJV). These statements express God's creative abilities and His desire that they flow to us and through us as we are drawn to Him by His loving-kindness. In *Creative Glory*, through Scripture and personal illustrations, Joshua Mills beautifully exposes this creative design and pattern of life—one that Jesus demonstrated for us when He was on earth and provides for us today.

—*Glenn Garland*
Calvary Pentecostal Tabernacle Camp, Ashland, VA

In an hour of great shaking, heaven invites the bride of Christ to walk in greater dimensions of God's glory. No one masterfully lays out a more biblical and adventurous road map packed with revelatory insights better than my dear friend Joshua Mills. Over the years, I have been influenced by his life and example of what it means to be a man consumed by the presence of Jesus. Joshua's new book, *Creative Glory*, is not just a must-have in your spiritual arsenal, but it is also a doorway into the creative-glory realm.

—*Torrey Marcel Harper*
Pastor, Habitation church
Senior Director and Founder, Global Prayer Room, New York City
Itinerant speaker, worship leader, and prophet
www.globalprayernyc.org

A dear friend and a gift to the body of Christ, Joshua Mills is a walking, talking epitome of living a life of creative glory. This heavenly reality has been passed down through the generations of his family, and Joshua has chosen this life-style, as well. He extends an invitation to all to enter into and exist in a higher realm. Creative glory *is possible* for those who choose to believe. Will you be one who is daring enough to attain the more, the greater with the Lord outside the four walls of the church? As you read *Creative Glory*, may the eternal, limitless God-dreams of your heart ignite to burn continually and produce lasting fruit that positively impacts this world while bringing a smile to the Father's face.

—*Courtenay Vandiver Pereira*
Classically trained cellist, psalmist, and creative arts teacher, Houston, Texas

CREATIVE
GLORY

Whitaker House Books and Resources by Joshua Mills

Angelic Activations

Power Portals: Awaken Your Connection to the Spirit Realm
Power Portals audiobook
Power Portals Study Guide

Moving in Glory Realms: Exploring Dimensions of Divine Presence
Moving in Glory Realms audiobook
Moving in Glory Realms Study Guide

Seeing Angels: How to Recognize and Interact with Your Heavenly Messengers
Seeing Angels audiobook
Seeing Angels Study Guide

7 Divine Mysteries: Supernatural Secrets to Unlimited Abundance
7 Divine Mysteries audiobook
7 Divine Mysteries Study Guide

Creative Glory: Embracing the Realm of Divine Expression
Creative Glory audiobook
Creative Glory Study Guide

Additional Audios
Activating Angels in Your Life
Experience His Glory
Healing from the Psalms
Opening the Portals
Prayer Power
Receive Your Healing
You Are Blessed

Devotional Resources
Activating Angels 365 (perpetual desktop calendar)
The Glory: Scriptures and Prayers to Manifest God's Presence in Your Life
Glory Bible Study: A Supernatural Exploration of the Word
The Power of His Names (77 devotional cards and guidebook)

CREATIVE GLORY

EMBRACING THE REALM OF DIVINE EXPRESSION

JOSHUA MILLS

WHITAKER
HOUSE

CREATIVE GLORY:
Embracing the Realm of Divine Expression

Joshua Mills
International Glory Ministries
JoshuaMills.com
info@joshuamills.com

ISBN: 978-1-64123-715-4 • eBook ISBN: 978-1-64123-716-1
Printed in the United States of America
© 2022 by Joshua Mills

Whitaker House
1030 Hunt Valley Circle
New Kensington, PA 15068
www.whitakerhouse.com

Library of Congress Control Number: 2021945789

1 2 3 4 5 6 7 8 9 10 11   ⊔⅃   29 28 27 26 25 24 23 22

DEDICATION

To my children, Lincoln, Liberty, and Legacy...my most beautiful and precious creations. Through your lives, I have seen, embraced, and enjoyed the beauty of heaven. Creative glory lives in you. I love you.

And to my spiritual children who read this book. Creative glory requires an open heart and a willing vessel. My prayer is that you would know the wonder of God and, through the revelation in this book, become a channel through which His creative glory can flow.

ACKNOWLEDGMENTS

To those who helped me in writing and publishing this book:

Harold McDougal
Lois Puglisi
Becky Speer
Christine Whitaker

To the creative team that captured the essence of creative glory in pictures:

Ryan West, photographer
Kim Appelt, creative director
Quentin Fears, stylist
Chaz Sanders, assistant to the photographer

To Sue Whitmire and the crew at Salvation Mountain, who granted us permission to shoot on location there.

To our Miracle Workers Partners, who continuously uphold the work of International Glory Ministries through their prayers and financial support.

Also, special thanks to Sid Krofft, Akiane Kramarik, and the late Leonard Knight for being a part of my own creative journey and graciously sharing yours with me.

Finally, to my wife, Janet Mills: huge thanks for all of your unending love and strength, which enabled me to release this book into the world.

"...for glory and for beauty."
—Exodus 28:2 (ESV)

CONTENTS

Foreword by Reba Rambo...21

Preface...23

PART I: WHAT IS CREATIVE GLORY?

1. The Spirit of Creativity...31
2. New Days and New Ways...45
3. Divine Expressions of Glory..61
4. The Creative Mind...77

PART II: THE FLOW OF CREATIVE GLORY

5. Awaken the Spirit Sound..95
6. Unlimited Flow...111
7. Angels of Creativity...127

PART III: ENTERING INTO CREATIVE GLORY

8. A Realm of Creative Miracles..149
9. Working Creative Miracles..169
10. Creative Connections...185
11. Creative Release...199

Conclusion: Creative Impartation...219

About the Author...223

FOREWORD

"Inspiration usually comes during work, rather than before it."
—*Madeleine L'Engle*

In our Genesis pattern, the Spirit (the essence and fullness) of the Divine Father was brooding, musing, swirling upon the face of the deep—not the shallow. Out of that Face-to-face relationship, and only then, came the creative command, "Let there be!"

When God looked into the glassy sea and saw His own reflection mirrored back to Him, He declared a resounding *Amen*: as in heaven, so be it on earth. Suddenly, the entire celestial realm burst forth into the song of beginnings. Why? Out of focused unity, limitless creativity is birthed.

I come from a long line of creatives. My family celebrated—and encouraged me to pursue—the arts of reading, studying, communicating, and listening to the Voice of the Universe. I was taught to believe I could see the unseen and trust that the Muse of heaven was guiding my yielded pen.

It is always a beautiful experience when God's breath stirs across my heart and the feathery mantle falls; but, more often than not, the creative process is just my showing up, doing the work, and trusting the Giver of the gift to guide my fragile hand. When we create, the Lord works with us—not apart from us.

Creative Glory, by my dear friend Joshua Mills, is all about receiving this celestial breath and guidance from God as we manifest His creativity in multiple ways in our lives. Joshua should always wear tennis shoes because he is forever running toward the glory and presence of Divine Wonder! Heaven's glory is his oxygen—his absolute, necessary atmosphere. He is born from above. Joshua has learned a vital secret: "Apart from Him, I can do nothing." And he passes along that secret to us in this book.

I believe *Creative Glory* will be an invaluable tool in your quest to understand more fully, and move more consistently in, higher dimensions of intimacy and relationship with the Glorious One. Thank you, Joshua, for paying the price for the precious oil of the anointing of *Creative Glory*.

—*Reba Rambo*

PREFACE

*"The Lord will create over the entire site of Mount Zion and over
her assemblies, a cloud by day, smoke, and the brightness of a flaming
fire by night; for over all the glory and brilliance will be a canopy
[a defense, a covering of His divine love and protection]."*
—Isaiah 4:5 (AMP)

When I was just a teenager, my maternal grandfather, Rev. Robert Degraw, gave me a book that changed my life. Books have a way of doing that if we allow them to. In that volume, I read words that described my own experiences in God as a Spirit-filled believer, and its lessons helped me to understand the spiritual journey that was still awaiting my discovery. The title of the book was *Glory: Experiencing the Atmosphere of Heaven*, and it was written by Ruth Ward Heflin. I've read that book countless times since then, and its message never seems to grow old. Actually, through the course of time, I feel as though I have absorbed its message into my life as a special impartation through the written word.

Although I never met Sister Ruth while she was here on earth, through the pages of her book, a divine connection was made between our lives in the spiritual realm. After she passed on to heaven, many of her close friends and contacts became friends of mine too—again by divine connection. Through these associations, I have increasingly experienced an ease in God's glory realm that has brought the purposes and timing of God for my life into fruition. Eventually, I also met members of Ruth Heflin's family. And, for well over a decade, Dr. Jane Lowder, Ruth's ministry successor, has invited me to minister at least twice a year at Calvary Pentecostal Tabernacle in Ashland, Virginia, the missions center founded by the Heflin family. Each time I stand in the pulpit there, I am amazed and honored by the way the Spirit imparts His revelation and wisdom to me. Never underestimate the power of words and what God can do in your life through reading and receiving the message of a book.

Of course, the most powerful book in the world is the Holy Bible, God's Word. Nothing can compare to the infallible truth and foundational wisdom that we receive as we study that living Word. But God's glory is without limitations, and the Spirit continues to lead men and women to write down the present-day revelation they receive from heaven. This revelation is not only for their benefit, but also for the benefit of others.

I have written this book in honor of the spiritual legacy of Ruth Ward Heflin. Through her writings, I have stepped into new territories of the Spirit and entered into new glory-realm awareness. From my own personal experiences and direct encounters in the Spirit, I have written new volumes about the glory, including this work. *Creative Glory* continues where Sister Ruth's books left off, for we go *"from glory to glory"* (2 Corinthians 3:18 KJVER, NKJV)!

In this book, you will discover fresh revelation and receive a new impartation to carry and release God's glory. The inspirational flow of the Spirit can shine God's light of hope into every situation and atmosphere on earth. It is always life-giving and full of great joy. When you are in the atmosphere of creative glory, you will think new thoughts and enter into an arena of heavenly ideas—the very environment of the heart and mind of God.

By our divine invitation to the ever-creative atmosphere of heaven, we can partner with the Lord to bring His manifest presence into the natural realm. Creative glory is available for God's people to flow together in unity to be carriers of His power, wisdom, and beauty.

My prayer is that the ongoing work of creative glory would continue to unfold for you. Creative glory presents us with the opportunity to realize the greatest possibilities in God that will move us forward as believers. It gives us the wisdom and provision of the heavenlies. It is our guarantee of future success. Creative glory is always unfolding and never withholding. Wherever we allow creative glory to flow, there will be a supernatural flourishing in every way.

CREATIVE GLORY IS ALWAYS UNFOLDING AND NEVER WITHHOLDING. INVITE GOD'S GLORY TO UNFOLD WITH CREATIVE SPLENDOR IN YOUR LIFE!

Recently, the Spirit spoke to me the following prophetic message about creative glory. May you be encouraged and inspired by these words to enter into God's creative glory and let that glory arise in you!

"I'm looking for a people, I'm calling forth a tribe,
I'm searching for creatives who in My glory thrive—
Those who would stand in the middle of My flame
And burn with a pure passion for My name,
Those who would embrace the golden dew from heaven
As My anointing is being released once again;
Those who would flow with My river,
Those who would blow with My wind,
Those who would release the oil of healing
As My Spirit rises from within.

"Oh yes, for My Spirit shall rise in this day,
And I shall rise on the scene
With creative patterns,
With creative sound,
With creative solutions and ideas,
With creative words and writings,
With creative expressions and art forms,

With creative blueprints and plans,
With creative dreams and visions,
With creative dance.

"And it will be in the last days," says God,
"That I will pour out My Spirit on all people;
Then your sons and your daughters will prophesy.
I will give voice to creative glory.
You will hear it!
Your young men will see visions,
And your old men will dream dreams.
I will give eyes to creative glory.
You will see it!
You will feel it!
You will taste it!
You will smell it!
You will know it!

"And through My creative glory,
I shall bring forth My people in a new way—
With creative miracles,
With creative song,
With creative signs and wonders.
With creative provisions, I will guide you along.

"It will be
A people with a new sound,
A people with a new dance,
A people with a new vision,
A people with a new radiance,
A people without aspirations of their own,
A people devoted to My glory,
With eyes fixed on My heavenly throne—
Not for fame or for personal power,
But for My name and the kingdom gospel
Being proclaimed in this hour.

"Creative glory
Shaping history,
Reclaiming identity,
Releasing purity.
Creative glory,
Divine ability,
Bringing maturity,
Opening the mystery with vibrant swirlings of love.

"Creative glory abounding in every way.
All that you need is in My glory, so just say,
'Creative glory! Let this glory arise in me!'"

PART I:

WHAT IS CREATIVE GLORY?

THE SPIRIT OF CREATIVITY

"In the beginning God created the heavens and the earth. The earth was formless and empty, and darkness covered the deep waters. And the Spirit of God was hovering over the surface of the waters."
—Genesis 1:1–2 (NLT)

*T*here's a wonderful, sixty-foot waterfall in Palm Springs, California, that I love to visit. It flows with pure water that streams down from the San Jacinto mountains from January until May. At the base of the waterfall, the water floods into a pool that is wide enough for a small group of people to swim in. You may ask me, "Why does the water only flow in the winter and spring months?" It's because the water has a particular source. That source is the fresh snow that falls upon the highest heights of the mountains. Eventually, that snow melts and descends as a refreshing stream that meanders down from the mountains and creates a beautiful desert oasis.

Everything has a source, including human creativity. Some people may feel that their ideas just seem to pop out of thin air, but that simply isn't the way it is. Every creative thought, impulse, expression, and motivation we have comes from some*where* and some*thing*. Just like the water that flows down from the mountains, creativity has a source, or starting point, where it all begins. The ultimate source of our human ability to create comes from the highest height known to mankind—the glory of God.

WHAT IS THE GLORY OF GOD?

Christians often speak about "the glory of God." But what is this glory? God's glory refers to the goodness, the fullness, and the splendor of His manifest presence. God's glory also has many other beautiful and wonderful facets that the Spirit desires to reveal to us, some of which we will explore throughout this book. God is the glory, and the glory is God!

In the Scriptures, the very first time we see the movement of God's glory, it is in a creative way: *"The Spirit of God was **hovering** over the surface of the waters."* God was preparing the atmosphere on earth to bring forth His heavenly dream of this world and its people.

All of creation declares God's glory:

The heavens are telling of the glory of God; and the expanse [of heaven] is declaring the work of His hands. (Psalm 19:1 AMP)

If we wanted to introduce someone to God for the first time, we could use many names, titles, and descriptions: God is eternal, without beginning or end. He is omniscient, or all-knowing; He is omnipotent, or all-powerful; and He is omnipresent, or fully present in all places at all times. The list could go on. But at the very beginning of the Bible, we are given a glimpse into the essence of who God is—we are introduced to His intrinsic nature as *Creator*: *"In the beginning God created."*

God is the Spirit of creativity! He Himself is the very essence of creativity. It was from God's own glory that heaven manifested its divine realities in the earthly realm. The Bible teaches us that every seed produces after its kind. (See Genesis 1:11–12.) Thus, there would be no human creators or creativity on earth if the Creator had not first given birth to creation from Himself. We were created in the image of God, the ultimate Creator. Therefore, we, too, have the ability to create, to invent, and to explore new possibilities. David expressed our wonderful creation by God when he sang this psalm to the Lord:

For you created my inmost being; you knit me together in my mother's womb. I praise you because I am fearfully and wonderfully made; your works are wonderful, I know that full well. (Psalm 139:13–14 NIV)

Thus, true human creativity is divinely inspired because it originates in God's glory realm, flowing to us and through us from the Creator. Some people might call this process "creative inspiration," but it's so much more than that because it comes from the very nature of God. I call it "creative glory."

God is the divine light and color that surround us.

He is the nucleus of splendid beauty.

He is the music.

He is all of creativity in its purest forms.

"Creative glory" refers to the physical and spiritual expressions of God's mind, heart, and emotions. God is eternal; therefore, when creative glory comes on the scene, the possibilities are endless, and the spiritual realms of opportunity are infinite.

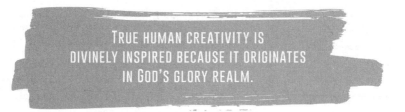

TRUE HUMAN CREATIVITY IS DIVINELY INSPIRED BECAUSE IT ORIGINATES IN GOD'S GLORY REALM.

RELEASING A CREATIVE DESTINY

God wants to pour out His creative glory upon us to reveal not only His beauty and innovations and possibilities, but also His truth. Through creative glory, we experience the freedom to learn and accept the truth about who we are in God. The Holy Spirit wants us to confront and discard any false ideas we have believed about ourselves or others. Once we begin to do this, we can build bridges and open power portals in the Spirit realm to help connect others with the divine wisdom and knowledge that we receive from Him.

One evening, before speaking at a Summer Campmeeting service in Ashland, Virginia, I called one of my precious prayer intercessors, "Momma"

Billie Deck. Momma Billie has often been with me in these camp meetings, but, this time, she was at home. I asked her, "Momma, would you pray for me before I go to minister at the camp this evening?"

She said yes and began to pray. As she did, she received revelation in the Spirit. This is what can happen in creative glory. As you lift your hands and your heart to God and find yourself lost in prayer, the spiritual seeing realm may open for you. You may see visions as God paints pictures before you and reveals to you His desires. The following is what God revealed to Momma Billie: she saw the hand of the Lord picking up a paintbrush and painting on the various people who would be present that night. God was releasing a creative destiny over our lives.

Then the picture changed, and she saw what she described as "an old-fashioned projector" with its reels turning. A light was coming out of the projector, and it seemed to be playing on the screen of our hearts. "Some of you," she said, "have felt lost or in an uncomfortable situation, and you didn't know how to move forward. God is going to shine His light on you tonight and show you things about your future. This will give you hope for that future. He will speak to you about your God-given destiny, about your specific assignment." This, she saw, would be projected onto the screen of our hearts as the glory of God brought divine revelation, confirmation, inspiration, and impartation. The creative glory of God would flow over us.

That night, it happened just as Momma Billie had said it would. As we gave more of ourselves to the Lord, He gave more of Himself to us. He made known the unknown to us. He opened our spirits to perceive and receive His plans for our lives. His creative glory moved in a new way; it was like a river flowing over us and like a fire burning within us. He sent the winds of His breath to sweep over us and change us more into His image. God desires to speak to us, but it is only through opening up to Him that we can truly attain the message that He is delivering. I believe that this will happen for you as you read this book with an open heart.

Another time, while hosting a special set of meetings in London, Ontario, I invited an artist named Kevin Moffat to come and paint during the worship sessions. Whenever Kevin stepped onto the platform, he would approach his easel with reverent awe toward God. In a prayerful, spiritually attentive attitude, he would then begin to touch the canvas with his paint-drenched fingers as he touched heaven with his heart. The most amazing thing about this approach was that, throughout the session, the inspired image he was producing became increasingly obvious. When the ministers preached, and prophetic words were released, the messages all aligned perfectly with the message that could be seen visibly forming in Kevin's art.

When an artist paints through the avenue of creative glory, each and every stroke of the brush is prophetic, and the colors are inspired. As the image emerges on the canvas, a download of revelation will suddenly appear before the eyes of, and in the heart of, the beholder.

> THERE WOULD BE NO HUMAN CREATORS OR CREATIVITY ON EARTH IF THE CREATOR HAD NOT FIRST GIVEN BIRTH TO CREATION FROM HIMSELF.

For artistic creators who yield themselves to creative glory, a profound spiritual experience unfolds:

For the visual artist, painting or drawing is worship.

For the chef, cooking is adoration.

For the musician, the expression of musical sound is sacred.

For the author, writing is an act of consecration.

For the dancer, each movement is filled with God's grace.

For the innovator, design and craftsmanship are holy things.

God can be found in the arts, for He is the ultimate and eternal Artist. And He can be found everywhere on earth, especially as His people allow Him to pour His creative glory into them and through them in their everyday lives. When did we come to the conclusion that true worship could only be offered within the confines of a church, temple, or tabernacle built by hands? True worship flows from the hearts of people who are open to give God the glory due to His name—no matter where they are and no matter what they are doing. Shouldn't we all live our lives in that way?

GOD'S MANIFOLD CREATIVITY

You might say, "But I'm not an artist. I'm not a singer. I'm not a musician. I'm not a painter. I'm not a writer. I don't do any of the 'creative things' you're talking about." Please understand that, even though many of the above examples are of various types of artists, when I speak of creative glory, I'm not just talking about God manifesting Himself through what we call the "creative arts." There is an entire, *multifaceted* dimension of creative glory that God wants to bring to you in a very personal way. It is specific to your life and giftings, and it is for the completion of your assignment in Him.

At their core, everyone is creative because they are patterned after their Creator. Whether you're aware of this ability or not is a different story altogether. Being creative comes naturally to some people, while others need more preparation and practice before they can get into a creative flow. If you need to stir up your creativity, then draw closer to your Creator and allow Him to express Himself through you. Learn how to open up a little more to the glory realm so that the Spirit can flow through your life with the unique abilities and perspectives He has given you.

Creative glory is a place where you can discover your true identity, callings, and giftings, and where you can feel embraced in your anointings. In this realm, it is given to you to be brave, to be bold, to break down barriers and walls of separation, to help and to heal. Creative glory comes not only to enable you to help and heal others, but also to help and heal *you*. Embrace this truth and allow it to come to fruition in your life.

God may download new inventions, new songs, new sounds, or new rhythms to your mind. He may speak to you about moving into a new occupation or finding new ways of doing your job better and more successfully. He may lead you to start a new business—guiding you in how to set it up and then develop it. He may reveal to you how to restore a broken relationship or give you creative ways to minister His love. He may show you new ways to flow in the glory. God is interested in prospering and blessing you!

When you come into contact with creative glory, you'll look at life through a different lens. And you will not only *see* what God is doing, but you will also *hear* it, *sense* it, *smell* it, and *taste* it. All the senses are involved. Creative glory makes you feel alive!

I believe this book is a divine connection for you into God's glory realm. Creative glory is a place where you will find solace and safety in His purposes for your life. Through its guidance, you may even find new community.

> WHEN YOU ARE IN THE ATMOSPHERE OF CREATIVE GLORY, YOU EXPERIENCE THE HEART AND MIND OF GOD!

"DREAMS ONLY WORK IF YOU DO"

For years, I've been saying that one of the most spiritual things I do is spend time with my family. And, within the safety of our family unit, I can really be me. I am free to enjoy, free to love, free to laugh, and free to give of myself to those whom God has given to me. When I'm with my family, I feel that I am my most creative self. Creative glory lives within me, and it also lives within my wife and children. The corporate presence that we experience when we're together brings so much peace to my heart. My wife, Janet, and I have taught our children to dream big and then to dream even bigger still!

Anyone who connects with creative glory will begin to dream big dreams. Creative glory pulls us up out of our self-constructed, limiting boxes and helps us recognize that there really were no boxes in our lives to begin with. The limitations we experience are man-made; but, in the Spirit realm, there are no limitations to what God can do in and through us, *"for God gives the [gift of the] Spirit without measure [generously and boundlessly]!"* (John 3:34 AMP).

However, Janet and I have also taught our children, "Dreams only work if you do." In other words, after you receive a God-given dream, idea, or plan, you must get up and *do* it! The impression you receive might seem unusual to you, and you might not know all that God has in mind for it, but when you obey Him, you—or future generations—will see His divine purposes unfold.

During the first few years that we lived in our previous residence (which we called *The Glory Manor,* always having a tendency to name our homes), I had an inspired idea to create a playroom for my children based on TV shows from my childhood. Although I was born in the late 1970s, I really grew up in the 80s, the golden era of Saturday-morning cartoons. When I was young,

I wanted to be an animator, so when I watched *The Jetsons* or *The Huckleberry Hound Show*, I noted every detail in my mind, and, once the program was finished, I would grab a pencil and pad of paper and attempt to sketch out every detail I could remember about the characters. One of the oldest pieces of artwork I have from my childhood is a brown paper grocery bag that I turned into a fabulous Fred Flintstone costume! I created it when I was five. My parents thought someone else must have helped me, but I had fashioned it all on my own.

I loved Hanna-Barbera cartoons then, and I still do, so I had the idea to turn the basement of our home into a "Hanna-Barbera Land." Anything is possible with God, and many things can be accomplished with a good imagination. Thankfully, I have both. Yet the way God fulfilled His purposes through that inspired idea was beyond anything I ever imagined.

First, I started planning out the space: I would construct a Flintstones area, complete with orange and black triangular curtains and lamp. We could use that area to watch movies. Beside that section, I would build an adult-sized ball pit with multicolored balls; there would be a large rainbow hovering over the top of it and cartoon characters dancing on the walls. It would be fun to incorporate an old coin-operated Dino ride, a Lucky Egg machine, and a Jetsons pinball machine. The empty space underneath the stairs could become a Yogi Bear cave. I would design a little entryway to crawl through the wall, and I would complete the cave with black-light paintings of Ranger Smith, Boo-Boo, Cindy Bear, and friends. The ideas were endless.

This is how creative glory works: when you give yourself to the Spirit in the glory realm, you suddenly find yourself in His creative flow. Sometimes there's so much flow that you can't turn it off. And why would you want to?

I bought the needed paint and pieces of plywood from my local hardware store. Then I went online and found old grocery-store amusements that were being sold at a great price. I searched high and low to find all the items I needed, and, little by little, my dream began to take shape.

While I was drawing and painting on the walls, my son, Lincoln, came down to the basement and asked, "Dad, why are you doing all this?" I told him that I had been inspired by an idea, and I wanted to run with it. Again, when creative glory comes on the scene, you have the choice to embrace the divine expression or reject it. I want to embrace creative glory in all areas of my life:

Creative glory inspires me to minister.

Creative glory leads me to write.

Creative glory gives me songs to sing.

Creative glory guides my whole life by divine light.

> WHEN YOU GIVE YOURSELF TO THE SPIRIT IN THE GLORY REALM, YOU WILL SUDDENLY FIND YOURSELF MOVING IN HIS CREATIVE FLOW.

PROACTIVELY CREATIVE

The Holy Spirit is the One who leads us into creative glory. Jesus declared,

But the Helper, the Holy Spirit, whom the Father will send in my name, he will teach you all things and bring to your remembrance all that I have said to you. (John 14:26 ESV)

If you need to know how to do something, the Holy Spirit has the revelation for it and wants to give that revelation to you. He is the Spirit of creativity. A spark of His inspiration is all you need to get started. That's it! Through the anointing of the Holy Spirit, you can receive the spark. The problem is that, in general, few people make the effort to fan the spark into a flame.

In writing about the spark of impartation that comes to us when the anointed hands of believers are placed upon our heads, Paul provided this godly advice to Timothy:

I remind you to fan into flame the gracious gift of God, [that inner fire— the special endowment] which is in you through the laying on of my hands [with those of the elders at your ordination]. For God did not give us a spirit of timidity or cowardice or fear, but [He has given us a spirit] of power and of love and of sound judgment and personal discipline [abilities that result in a calm, well-balanced mind and self-control]. (2 Timothy 1:6–7 AMP)

When creative glory comes to us, we must fan the flame of divine inspiration. Once more, this means taking practical steps—putting into action the visions that have been impressed upon our hearts. As I wrote previously, at times, we don't understand the reasons why we are being led to do something, much like an artist often doesn't know what the end-result of their creation will look like. But in order to arrive at an end result, you must be willing to show up, face the blank canvas, put paint on the brush, so to speak, and begin to create. This is faith in motion. Creative glory requires faith, and faith is revealed through action.

Eventually, my inspiration for Hanna-Barbera Land came into full manifestation in our basement at The Glory Manor. The result was even better than I had first envisioned it would be. In God's purposes, that playroom became a place of ministry and fellowship. We often invited other families over to our home, and, as the children jumped among the balls and played with the arcade games, we were able to pray with and minister to the parents. We held birthday parties in that room, and our teenage son and his friends enjoyed hanging out there more than anywhere else.

A few years after I created the playroom, my father was diagnosed with cancer and underwent medical treatment. During that difficult time, my mother would crawl into the Yogi Bear cave, having turned it into her own special and anointed prayer closet. It became a secret place for her. In that cave, amid the sparkling gems and accompanied by an animatronic bear, Mom poured her heart out to the Lord, and He heard her. There, many tears flowed, prayers were answered, and healing came. It was a little miracle realm. When I started that project, little did I know just how important the cave would become to my family and friends.

When creative glory is in operation, the Spirit leads us to do things we've never done before, and we must be willing to say yes and then attempt to do them with His guidance. Creative glory opens new pathways for us that we must travel. When you begin moving with an inspired idea, you may experience some criticism, harsh words, or ridicule from people who lack the revelation of what you're doing. Don't take this opposition to heart. You are responsible only for your own journey, your own personal response to God's leading.

For many years, Janet and I have anointed pieces of cloth by placing our supernaturally oil-soaked hands on them and praying in faith for the lost to be saved, the sick to be healed, and those who were oppressed by the enemy to be delivered. When these cloths were distributed to people, God worked miracles. This is a scriptural practice; in the book of Acts, we see people being healed and delivered through anointed pieces of clothing that had been in contact with the apostle Paul:

> *God did extraordinary miracles through Paul, so that even handkerchiefs and aprons that had touched him were taken to the sick, and their illnesses were cured and the evil spirits left them.* (Acts 19:11–12 NIV)

A few years ago, the Spirit gave me a creative idea for ministering powerful healing to the sick in a similar yet new way. When I was preparing to release my book *Moving in Glory Realms*, I was considering different items that I might include in a gift box to send to influencers to help promote the new book. I wanted to include items that were meaningful and also conveyed the idea of movement. I believe that the Spirit dropped into my spirit the idea of including socks in the gift box. The more I thought about it, the stronger the conviction grew within me that I should do this. I could design these socks with various colors that carried prophetic meaning, and people could wear them as a reminder that, as they "walked by faith," the Spirit walked with them. I was able to find a company in Austin, Texas, that would work with me to create these socks, and the supernaturally inspired idea was given birth.

Although they were only meant as a limited-run promotional item, these socks became extremely popular. People began calling our ministry office specifically asking for them. They had found that they could use them as a spiritual point of contact, very much in the same way we anointed cloths as a touchpoint for ministry. They could pray over the socks and give them away to those who were most in need of a miracle.

Then I felt the Spirit leading me to produce another pair of socks that I would call "Walking in Healing." They would be designed in a beautiful green color representing new growth, new life, new beginnings, and wholeness. The socks would have seven healing Scriptures on them. In this way, those who wore them could be continually reminded of God's healing promises from His Word.

When we first made these socks available, we sold out within days. I believe the demand was great because, to my knowledge, we were offering something that nobody else had before. Since that time, almost every week, we have received testimonies from people who have worn the socks or given them to loved ones, and experienced wonderful healing miracles. The socks were, and continue to be, a great success. Yet we've also experienced a degree of resistance and negativity from people who haven't understood our motives and intentions for making the socks available.

We can't expect that everybody will understand the ways in which creative glory leads us. However, we cannot afford to ignore a supernatural invitation from the glory realm. Although there are risks involved, seeing the higher purposes of God unfold is worth every sacrifice. Creative glory requires our sensitivity to receive from the Spirit and our willingness to release what He gives us into the earthly realm. Although we only see in part (see 1 Corinthians 13:12), our Father knows the end from the beginning (see Isaiah 46:10), and He starts with the end in mind. How wonderful that we can trust His process!

As I will discuss further in chapter 2, creative glory helps us to solve difficult problems and gives us new ways of supplying needs and fixing longstanding issues. It leads us to be innovators—and remember that most, if not all, innovators have been misunderstood at some point. It has been said, "It's lonely at the top," but I want to give you a better vantage point. It's all about perspective. Although it's easy to feel isolated, you must remember that God and His angels are always with you, and He wants to be the reason you do what you do.

Let me strongly encourage you: *actively determine to get into the flow of God.* When you do, all limits will vanish, and you will stop saying things like the following: "I can't!" "It's not an option!" "I've never done that!" "It's beyond my reach!" Vincent van Gogh wrote, "If you hear a voice within you say 'you cannot paint,' then by all means paint and that voice will be silenced."[1]

I believe the Lord is saying to us, "Be bold! Take off the limits and let My creative glory flow into you, around you, and through you." Heaven's intention is that you succeed in fulfilling your God-given destiny and purpose.

ACTIVELY DETERMINE TO GET INTO THE FLOW OF GOD.
LET CREATIVE GLORY FLOW!

---

1. "Vincent Van Gogh Quotes," Vincent Van Gogh, https://www.vincentvangogh.org/quotes.

GOD'S LIGHT OF HOPE AND JOY

Creative glory is the wisdom of the heavenlies and our guarantee of future success. Remember, the inspirational flow of creative glory shines the light of hope into every situation and atmosphere we are in. Even now, a new joy in the Holy Spirit is being released to strengthen you spiritually, emotionally, and physically. God's joy will fill you completely, from the top of your head all the way down to the tips of your toes. You will be so filled with joy that you will overflow with creative expression!

Again, wherever we allow creative glory to flow, there will be a supernatural flourishing in every way. God wants to lead us by His creative glory!

CREATIVE GLORY! LET THIS GLORY ARISE IN ME!

NEW DAYS AND NEW WAYS

"Behold, I am doing a new thing; now it springs forth,
do you not perceive it? I will make a way in
the wilderness and rivers in the desert."
—Isaiah 43:19 (ESV)

Authors are frequently asked how they began writing books or where they got the inspiration to write a particular book. I first started writing by simply putting my thoughts about worship ministry onto the page. I had been asked by my pastor to teach an afternoon worship workshop, and I felt it would be good to have notes in bullet-point form that I could hand out to the participants. Those few notes eventually turned into a small worship manual. Taking that initial step gave me enough confidence to believe I could write a book that was a bit longer. My next project was a compilation of personal testimonies of supernatural works God had done in my own life and within the life of my church community. At that time, I wasn't a preacher, and I didn't speak at large conferences. I simply had personal experiences with God that I wanted to share with others. Eventually, as I continued to write books and also record albums, those works found their way to the right people in the right places, giving them more widespread reach. And, through a supernatural progression, doors eventually opened for me to preach and sing on some of the most honored platforms, ministering to God's people all over the world.

It's always been amazing to me how my books and songs have traveled to places I could never reach in the natural. Creative glory will make a way, carrying your creative works into the places and to the people that need them most. Over the years, I've written more than thirty books and spiritual training manuals. I've also worked on dozens of recording projects as well as personal art projects, such as drawing, painting, doing animation, and creating films.

I can't remember a time in my life when I wasn't creative, and yet I realize that the creativity I have operated in all these years has not been natural. Rather, it has been supernaturally given by the Spirit. As you read about my experiences in this chapter, I encourage you to receive the supernatural impartation of creative glory in your own life.

CREATIVE PROPHETIC GUIDANCE

My mother gave me the name *Joshua* before I was born. While she was still pregnant with me, she was instructed by the Spirit to sit down at her typewriter and write out a message, which was a prophetic word for her. The Lord told her that she was carrying a son in her womb and that she should name him Joshua, after Joshua in the Bible, who was a leader of God's people.

The Spirit told Mom many other things, among them that the enemy would try to harm her baby but that she shouldn't be afraid, just as the Lord had said to the leader Joshua: *"Do not fear or be dismayed (intimidated)"* (Joshua 8:1 AMP). Mom typed out the full message, put it into an envelope, and kept it as a very personal, prophetic word from the Lord. God knew that she would need that word in coming months and years.

My parents were part of a very talented gospel music group called The New Covenant Children. Both of my parents sang, and my father played the drums. They were actually singing the night my mother's water broke. On their way to church that evening, Mom had told Dad, "This is the last time I'll be singing before our baby is born!" This announcement came as a surprise to him because it was only January, not the time in the natural for me to be born. I was scheduled to arrive a few months later, in March.

Because I was a first child, it might have been natural for my ᵖ be fearful when I showed up earlier than expected. In recent years, knowledge about caring for premature babies has greatly advanced, and ing technologies have been developed to save the lives of newborns. In the late 1970s, the technology was not nearly as advanced, and preemies often died. But Mom says that when I was whisked away by doctors to the neonatal intensive care unit of the hospital, she did not feel one pang of fear for my life. She had the prophetic word of the Lord, His promise for my future, to hold on to.

Over the years, I have asked my mother several times about the circumstances of my premature birth and how she dealt with it. She has insisted that what the Spirit showed her at the typewriter that day was so convincing she never had a single moment of anxiety about the circumstances. Others were worried, but she remained calm through it all.

STANDING FIRM

I want you to understand a vital truth: regardless of where you are in life, regardless of what you are currently going through, and regardless of what you see in the physical world, you have God's Word to stand on. In Jeremiah 29:11, we read, "'For I know the plans I have for you,' says the LORD. 'They are plans for good and not for disaster, to give you a future and a hope'" (NLT). That is God's promise, and it is His *rhema* word to you today, meaning that it applies to your circumstances as you receive it. Grab hold of it and hang on to it in the days to come. You may need to print or write out by hand Jeremiah 29:11 and place it where you can see it frequently. Whenever you start to dwell on a negative situation, it will remind you not to worry about what you see in the natural. God knows the plans He has for you, and He will be faithful to fulfill those plans.

Don't be concerned about the heaviness and oppression permeating our world. Watching or reading the news these days can actually make one physically ill. In the realms of evil, a swirling funnel of wickedness is threatening our well-being. However, instead of focusing on the problems, which can suck you down into a mire of hopelessness, you need to pray in the Spirit, read the Bible, and proclaim the Word of God over your life. The heavens are open within us, and we have access to the Creator of the universe. Creative glory is available for you to see new ways to do things that others have not yet seen.

God wants to release through you what you have never thought of before, what you didn't even realize was possible.

Don't think for a moment that God hasn't considered the national and international situations we currently face. There is a lot of debate going on today about what's right and what's wrong, what's true and what's false. I can tell you this: the Holy Spirit is the Spirit of truth, and He has promised to lead us into all truth. (See John 16:13.) When you speak God's truth, you give permission for the Spirit to guide you. God wants His creative glory to flow through you with His truth. As that glory flows through you, others will see it, receive wisdom and help by it, and give praise to God for it.

The days we are living in right now are very challenging, yet they are also intriguing because finding solutions to the unique problems we face requires a new way of thinking, a new way of walking, a new way of doing things, a new way of living. God wants to give these solutions to His people. He wants to lift us up through His Spirit! With God, there is a better way, a heavenly way, a creative way to live—and we can find this way in the glory.

When you are in Christ, you can be sure that things are not falling apart. (See, for example, Colossians 1:17.) The truth is: things are falling into place. We try in our own ability to do great feats, but we fail. We try to "program" the Spirit, which never works. We organize circumstances without the Spirit, but we see no fruit, no success. We must allow the Lord Himself to build our marriages, families, businesses, careers, and everything else in our lives. If we don't allow Him to do this, if we try to build our lives through our own efforts, we *"labor in vain"* (Psalm 127:1 KJVER). But when we allow God to do His work, and His creative glory flows through us, He will surely surprise us with the wondrous result!

Rather than days filled with gloom, these can be days of great opportunity. Rise up, child of God. This is your day!

WHEN YOU SPEAK GOD'S TRUTH, YOU GIVE PERMISSION FOR THE SPIRIT TO GUIDE YOU.

A REALM FOR THE NEW

For years, church leaders have talked a lot about God bringing "the new" to us. We have been preaching, prophesying, teaching, and singing about "the new." "Lord," we said, "we want 'the new.' God, give us 'the new.'" We love Isaiah 43:19:

Behold, I am doing a new thing; now it springs forth, do you not perceive it? I will make a way in the wilderness and rivers in the desert. (ESV)

Creative glory creates an atmosphere for "the new" in our lives. It turns on divine lights in our hearts and minds! In "the new," we see what we have never seen before, and we taste what we have never tasted before. We are able to embrace the expressions of glory that come to reveal Jesus to us and to the world around us.

When we are in an atmosphere of creative glory, suddenly, strong impressions are imprinted upon our hearts, and ideas pop into our heads that we've never had before. A *"new thing"* comes to us to make a new way. Creative glory presents the opportunity for us to enter into greater possibilities in God, and this is a provision we all need.

Of course, we can't do all of that in our own strength. Again, it will be accomplished only through the Holy Spirit who lives inside us. He is the Waymaker, and He will make a way for God's creative purposes to come forth on earth.

In Deuteronomy 28:12, God declares,

The LORD will open to you his good treasury, the heavens, to give the rain to your land in its season and to bless all the work of your hands. And you shall lend to many nations, but you shall not borrow. (ESV)

"You shall lend to many nations, but you shall not borrow." Wow! How can we do that? Through creative glory. God wants His people to be the head, not the tail. He wants us to go up, not down. He wants us to be on the top, not the bottom:

And the LORD will make you the head and not the tail, and you shall only go up and not down, if you obey the commandments of the LORD your God, which I command you today, being careful to do them.

(Deuteronomy 28:13 ESV)

We are called to be spiritual pioneers, making a way in the spiritual and physical realms where there has previously been no way. God is ready to create something new in you and around you. Are you ready for it?

INTUITIVE CREATIVITY

Creative glory brings the new by causing us to experience self-discovery and personal awakening. In Ecclesiastes 3:11, we are told that God *"has also planted eternity [a sense of divine purpose] in the human heart [a mysterious longing which nothing under the sun can satisfy, except God]"* (AMP). In this eternal purpose, we are connected directly to creative glory.

From the time I was very young, I have felt this creative connection in my life. In many ways, I was just like other children; however, there were some early signs of the creative leadership I would mature into.

For example, during the summer months, when my friends and I were bored and had nothing to do, I would spice things up by conceiving some creative activities and enthusiastically making them a reality. We didn't have much money, so my activities were low-budget—like the time I went from house to house rounding up all the neighborhood kids for a parade.

Everyone gathered in my backyard, and we created floats by decorating our wagons, tricycles, and bicycles with bits and pieces of anything we could find. I then went through the closets in our home and pulled out whatever could be used for costumes. The other kids ran home to get costumes from their houses as well. We all dressed up as anything and everything we could imagine. And then the parade began.

We started at my house, which was at one end of the street, and paraded all the way down to the other end of the street. Then we turned around and paraded all the way back. Neighbors came out of their homes and clustered along the street, amused to see their children marching by, dressed as many different silly characters and singing their hearts out while playing tambourines and drums. What a wonderful time we had that day!

As soon as one boredom-relieving activity like the parade was over, another idea would come to my mind. I would gather my neighborhood friends for another escapade—and it went on that way. We created neighborhood circuses, put on puppet shows, sold tickets to a backyard theme park, made a candy store in our playhouse, and even went door-to-door selling b bouquets of dandelions and other wildflower arrangements. The creative ideas were endless! I know now that this was all part of the call God had placed on my life. At the time, I didn't realize that what I was doing was bringing people together. There was a wonderful unity to our many adventures. I also didn't realize how much joy we were bringing to the neighborhood. Our antics always seemed to make people feel better. Creative glory was flowing even in my young life.

This creative flow is in my generational stream. My great-grandfather, Neil Degraw, built a full-sized merry-go-round on his front lawn for the enjoyment of the neighborhood children. His home was not very big, so when the merry-go-round was fully functioning, his house got lost behind it. A carpenter by trade, Great-grandfather had built the merry-go-round by hand and decorated it with nursery rhyme scenes that my Aunt Roseanna painted for him. He had learned to be a builder while he was in the army, but creative glory was the source of his inspiration. For music, Great-grandfather played my parents' gospel records.

I remember happily riding on that merry-go-round many times while eating a bowl of ice cream that Great-grandfather had given me to enjoy at the same time. The merry-go-round brought much delight not only to the children of the neighborhood but also to the whole community. When an overburdened local minister who needed encouragement would come to visit, Great-grandfather would tell him, "What you need is a nice ride on the merry-go-round!" Then he would escort the man of God to the amusement ride— with a bowl of ice cream, of course. After circling around a few times while listening to the gospel records and eating his ice cream, the minister would feel much better!

God has many ways of bringing personal and spiritual refreshment to people. He wants to bring a flow of His creative ideas into *your* life, too, so that it can spill over to others. Whether or not you felt a connection to creative glory at an early age like I did, God has placed His creativity within you by His Spirit. Receive it! Again, the creative ideas you receive in the glory realm might cause you to do unusual things in unusual ways. But that's okay, because they will also bring unity, great joy, and refreshment.

> GOD IS READY TO CREATE
> SOMETHING NEW IN YOU AND AROUND YOU.
> ARE YOU READY FOR IT?

GLORY-INSPIRED IDEAS

In Scripture, many times, when God's glory is revealed, we see Him in action as the Creator. As I mentioned in chapter 1, just as the glorious Spirit of God hovered over the surface of the deep when He prepared to create the masterpiece of planet Earth, the Spirit of God comes to us today with many creative expressions. Consider His creativity in making humanity: God created the first human, Adam, from the dust of the ground. Using another unusual method, He created Eve from one of Adam's ribs.

It is best to be open to however God wants to infuse us with His creative-glory ideas. When we are in the atmosphere of His glory, a free flow of heavenly innovations may be downloaded into our spirits. For instance, sometimes, when I am lost in worship, God will suddenly speak to my heart regarding an answer I had been seeking. Or I might be at the altar giving myself to prayer and yielding to the Spirit of God or soaking in the Spirit on the floor, and God will speak to my spirit, enabling me to sense or know something new. When creative ideas arise within us by God's Spirit, that is creative glory at work.

At the beginning of creation, God said, *"Let there be light,"* and the entire universe was illuminated in an instant. (See Genesis 1:3, various translations.) Creative glory allows us to see what has never been seen before. And it can also help us to recover something that has been hidden for a long time. For instance, it will highlight the Scriptures for us in a new and vibrant way. How many times have you read the same verse over and over and over again, and each time it has meant the same to you? But, one day, you sensed the manifest glory of God upon you. When you read that Scripture again, this time, it took on a whole new meaning. The light was turned on, and you saw something in the Word that you had never noticed before. This happens to me all the time.

God wants to take us all deeper into His heart and mind. He is the Spirit of revelation, and He wants to bring revelation to you. There is so much more to Him and to His kingdom than what may be seen on the surface. Likewise, there is much more to your life than what you or others see on the surface. You need to dig a little deeper in God and be open to receive His revelation.

UNPLUG...REBOOT...RESET!

The Lord often uses our life circumstances to bring us into a greater level of knowing His faithfulness and goodness. But to receive the new that God wants to give us, we must allow Him to "reset" our lives.

A few months ago, Lincoln was trying to do something on the Internet at home. I was in the office on the other side of the wall, and he yelled through to me, saying that he couldn't get the Internet to work. I called out the password to him, but he said he had tried that already. I thought for a moment and then suggested that he unplug the router, let it rest a few minutes, and then plug it in again. Often, rebooting electronic equipment will do the trick, and it worked for him that day.

A few days later, I was trying to make toast in the kitchen, but, for some reason, when I pressed down the lever on the toaster, the bread would not go down. Remembering how the Internet equipment had needed to be rebooted, I unplugged the toaster, waited a little while, and then plugged it in again. This time it worked as it should.

A few days after that, I was working in the office again, and the printer wouldn't work. The computer was sending files to the printer, but it was not responding. By this time, I had fully received the revelation: turn it off, let it rest a few minutes, and then turn it on again. When I did that, the printer soon began cranking out pages. The power of rebooting is wonderful! Apparently, many things can be fixed by rebooting. You have probably received the same revelation.

Recognizing this principle made me think of the worldwide coronavirus pandemic. It is obvious that the enemy wanted to use this time of crisis for his destructive purposes, especially in causing people to feel fearful. (Contrast Luke 12:4.) But God gives us creative glory to overcome every evil intention of the enemy, including those on a global scale.

Although the enemy tried to bring a curse, to bring destruction, to bring trouble, to bring atrocities, and to cause the lives of many to collapse, God was using the situation to offer believers in Him a new opportunity. He was releasing something new to us so that it could flow through us in a creative way.

When the pandemic began, suddenly, much about the way we lived became different. God did not cause the virus. But I believe He used the quarantines, restrictions, and shortages to bring some of the newness into our lives that we had been seeking. Even during this difficult and painful time in which many people became ill and suffered loss, God was allowing people to use their circumstances to grow in their ability to be creative and innovative—not only to survive or to maintain their lives, but also to develop brand-new ideas and ways of doing things that would better their own lives and the lives of others. And yet, we sometimes cursed the inconvenience rather than seeking how God would have us respond to it. We said, "God, what is happening? What's going on? I don't like this. I don't feel very comfortable with this whole situation." But creative glory comes to turn difficult situations around for our good.

After much personal suffering, Joseph expressed this truth to his brothers who had sold him into slavery:

> As for you, you meant evil against me, but God meant it for good.
> (Genesis 50:20 ESV)

In our troubled world, and even in the body of Christ, there is much disorder and dysfunction, but this doesn't have to be the case. God has a way of unplugging us from ungodly practices and unhealthy associations, giving us a short rest for refreshment, and then plugging us in again—this time, to work and live as we were intended to. He is doing something new that will cause us to function at a higher capacity. It is important to remember that, in God, there is never loss. As long as we have creative glory, we can face whatever comes our way.

Creative glory has taught me to sow my setbacks as seeds in order to receive a harvest of setups. I do this by letting go of the past, continuing to seek God and His revelation, obeying His Word, giving thanks in all circumstances, and showing His compassion to others. When we are in the glory, our God will turn what seems to be a bad situation into a glorious one. As believers in Christ, we are always at an advantage. We always have the upper hand over the enemy. We often say that we are *"more than conquerors"* (Romans 8:37 ESV, AMP, KJVER, NIV) in Christ, but do we really believe this truth?

> CREATIVE GLORY HAS TAUGHT ME
> TO SOW MY SETBACKS AS SEEDS IN ORDER TO
> RECEIVE A HARVEST OF SETUPS.

God's workmanship is marvelous, and He has placed His Spirit of creativity inside *you* so you can create marvelous things and do innovative works on earth. As creative glory flows through you, God can give you divine solutions for problems, original thoughts and ideas no one else has ever had. Get ready for an explosion of creative glory to burst onto the scene in these days!

Yes, God wants to do this for *you*. He wants to show *you* a creative way to educate your children. He wants to give *you* a creative way to earn an honest and living wage. He wants to give *you* a creative way for finances to flow into your life. He is not satisfied when you have just enough to get by. His will for you is abundance. He not only wants you to pay your bills, but He also wants you to be an overflowing blessing everywhere you go. He may give you a business idea that will help to support the proclamation of the gospel. Such ideas will flow to those who are open and willing to receive them. All you need to do is reach up in the glory and take hold of them. Let go of all doubt, let faith arise, and allow God's creative solutions to come forth.

HEAVENLY STRATEGIES

When you immerse yourself in the Spirit, God will send you heavenly strategies, such as the strategy that gave Joshua victory over the city of Jericho. What was the strategy God gave him? It was unusual, for sure, but Joshua obeyed. Joshua and the Israelites were to walk around the city once a day for six days. Then, on the seventh day, they were to walk around the city seven times. On the seventh time around, the priests were to blow the shofar. When they did that, the walls would come tumbling down. (See Joshua 6:1–21.)

If Joshua had told carnally minded people this plan, they would have laughed at him and said it could never happen. But whatever God speaks *must* happen. Therefore, if we listen to the voice of God and act accordingly, creative glory will intervene to lead us into our greatest victories. In creative glory, God places His *"super*-ability" on our *natural* ability, and this is the way it becomes *supernatural* capacity. Let the Spirit's *"extra"* anoint your *ordinary*, making it *extraordinary*.

When Paul and Silas were in prison, it looked like they were at a disadvantage. They had done nothing wrong; instead, they had been imprisoned for doing good. What did God show them to do? He led them to sing His praises and loudly call on His name—right there in the prison. When they did that, creative glory worked for them. The ground shook, their chains fell off, and the doors of the prison opened wide. Not only were Paul and Silas set free, but the jailer and his entire family were saved. (See Acts 16:16–33.)

Remember, when creative glory flows through you, it does not only benefit you, but it also causes a blessing to flow out to others. A blessing will flow throughout your city, your region, and your nation. Why? Because you have chosen to move with the Spirit of God, who is the Spirit of creativity. Creative glory positions and equips us with the heavenly tools for whatever we need to do. We read in Psalm 51:

> *Create in me a clean heart, O God, and renew a steadfast spirit within me. Do not cast me away from Your presence, and do not take Your Holy Spirit from me. Restore to me the joy of Your salvation, and uphold me by Your generous Spirit.* (Psalm 51:10–12 NKJV)

David prayed this prayer long before he knew of the provision of salvation that comes for each of us through Jesus Christ. Today, under the new covenant, we might pray David's prayer differently. We might start out the same, saying, "God, create a clean heart in me, and renew a right spirit within me." But then we might pray, "Lord, thank You that, because of Jesus, I can live in Your presence, and You will not remove Your Spirit from me. Restore to me the joy of Your salvation. Bring me back to my first love." (See Revelation 2:4.)

As we have discussed, life has become very complicated and confusing for many believers today; there is far too much clutter in our lives, weighing us down and distracting us from God's purposes. Creative glory gets rid of the clutter and brings us back to the basics as it enables us to bless others. David prayed, *"Then I will teach transgressors Your ways, and sinners shall be converted to You"* (Psalm 51:13 NKJV).

Creative glory helps us to get back on track. Sometimes, when we've been moving in one direction without good results, God will say, "Come back to Me, and I will run the race with you and take the victory lap with you. Come and do what you were called to do before you were born." Our good intentions for our lives on earth may be nice, but God's intentions for our lives are supernatural and eternal. God wants to give us His intentions so we will flow with His creative glory.

My dear friends Pastors Joe and Bella Garcia are very joyful, Spirit-filled people, and they have a saying, "If it's not fun, we don't want it." Although, every day, we are in a very real spiritual battle, we must always remember, first and foremost, that the joy of the Lord provides us with supernatural strength to overcome and win. (See Nehemiah 8:10.) Some believers walk around with a very sad countenance. They have succumbed to fear that has been compounded by negative media reports and so-called experts in various fields regarding the dire state of the world and its future. But there is no need for fearfulness. God has given us the upper hand! He has placed us in positions of victory because His glory is filled with joy! God has already determined our success. We only need to choose to live in the flow of His creative glory.

SEEDS OF GLORY

Creative glory is a seed. If we receive it and plant it by faith, obedience, and seeking God, it will grow. Soon, it will blossom and bear fruit:

And in the last days it shall be, God declares, that I will pour out my Spirit on all flesh, and your sons and your daughters shall prophesy, and your young men shall see visions, and your old men shall dream dreams; even on my male servants and female servants in those days I will pour out my Spirit, and they shall prophesy. (Acts 2:17–18 ESV)

This Scripture passage speaks about the creative flow that comes when the Spirit of God arrives on the scene. Creative glory brings the "new" of God by doing all of the following—and much more:

+ Releasing dreams and visions

+ Opening the seeing realm

+ Removing blinders

+ Eliminating negativity and darkness
+ Opening our eyes to the light of God's glory
+ Revealing God's creative ability and ideas
+ Renewing our spirits
+ Encouraging us
+ Bringing the joy of God's presence to us
+ Generating miracles in, for, and through us
+ Accelerating the purposes of the Spirit in our lives

I pray that you will embrace the realms of creative glory flowing into your life because, as you do, divine expression will be released through you! From this day forward, may a flow of creative glory surround you. May God show you a creative way to be a better spouse, a better parent, a better minister, a better employee, a better business owner, a better student, a better artist—creative ways to do whatever God has called you to do for His glory.

I declare that your eyes are open to see in the Spirit, and you will have heavenly visions. Your mind is open to perceive in the Spirit, and you will have spiritual dreams. Your mouth is open to prophesy the word of the Lord, and, by that word, you will create and recreate in the natural realm what God has already given you in the supernatural realm. Let the glory flow!

CREATIVE GLORY! LET THIS GLORY ARISE IN ME!

3

DIVINE EXPRESSIONS OF GLORY

*"Let the beauty of the L*ORD *our God be upon us, and establish the work of our hands for us; yes, establish the work of our hands."*
—Psalm 90:17 (NKJV)

Out in the California desert, an hour and a half east of Palm Springs, past the Salton Sea, there is a wondrously surprising site: a Dr. Seuss-like dreamworld that seemingly springs up from the ground with rainbows of Technicolor adobe mounds. This site is called Salvation Mountain, and it's the lifework and achievement of a spiritual dreamer and folk artist named Leonard Knight.

GOD IS LOVE

Janet and I had the privilege of meeting Leonard many years ago when we first heard about this unusual tourist attraction and decided to take my parents, who were visiting us in California, on a daylong adventure. When we arrived at Salvation Mountain, it really was quite a sight to see: a small, man-made mountain rising vibrantly under the golden sunshine, with the striking words "God Is Love" boldly painted on front, underneath a tall, white cross standing proudly on top. Below those bold words was a large red heart. Inside the heart was the Scripture reference of Acts 2:38 and Leonard's own version of the sinner's prayer:

"Jesus, I'm a sinner. Please come upon my body and into my heart."

This hand-painted wonder was intriguing, inspiring, and, we discovered, unplanned!

When we arrived that day at Salvation Mountain, we were the only ones there except for Leonard, whose hands were covered in paint. He was busy working away on a new portion of his masterpiece. Leonard was happy to see us; he was excited that we had come to visit him and his art, and even more excited to show us around and tell us his story. He explained that he had never set out to build a tourist attraction; he had only wanted to share the message of God's love with people.

We learned that, in 1967, in Southern California, Leonard Knight and his sister had given their lives to Jesus Christ. After this life-changing experience, Leonard was set ablaze with a passion to win the lost. Carrying a strong evangelistic anointing, he had such a desire to be a soulwinner that most churches he tried to join had no idea what to do with him. In 1970, a bit frustrated, feeling stifled in his call, and knowing that there had to be a way to spread the message of God's love without resistance, Leonard had a grandiose idea: he could put the message "God Is Love" on a hot-air balloon and fly it all over America and even around the world! So, he drove across the country looking for people who would financially support his vision, but he came up short. Nevertheless, he was sure he would find a way. Creative glory was still at work!

While Leonard was in Nebraska, he was led to a source of scrap balloon fabric. He spent the next few years collecting the odd pieces he could gather while learning how to sew and piecing together the swatches. The homemade hot-air balloon began to look like Joseph's coat of many colors. Leonard saw it as a wonder to behold!

Leonard worked on that hot-air balloon for sixteen long years, taking odd jobs here and there to be able to purchase extra pieces of fabric. But after all that work and all those years, he was—quite literally—never able to get his vision off the ground. With time, the material he was using began to rot and rip because of the summer humidity and the winter dampness. Leonard's dream was dead...or so he thought.

A COLORFUL IDEA

Leonard went through a period of disappointment, truly believing that he would never be able to share the message of God's love to the extent he desired. (I think many creatives go through such seasons, but we must never give up.) Leonard told us that, feeling overwhelmingly defeated, he moved to the California desert to run away from his problems. Yet, when he arrived in Slab City, he got another idea. This time, he thought he might create a monument to convey God's love. He carried half a bag of cement up a hillside, intending to build something small and then leave. But once he started working on this new project, he just couldn't bring himself to leave it. He continued building the mound higher and higher, adding sand to the cement mixture in order to stretch his limited supply, all the while painting and decorating his creation. Yet, after more than three years of sacrifice and hard work, his plans failed miserably once again when the entire structure collapsed!

To most people, this setback would have been totally disheartening, but Leonard was determined to succeed. He studied new ways to apply and sculpt the desert's natural adobe, and he built a totally new structure, working on it over the next thirty years. The result is a 50-foot adobe mountain covered with 300,000 gallons of hand-painted waterfalls, rivers, flowers, bluebirds, and Bible verses. As I mentioned previously, this piece of art has come to be known as "Salvation Mountain." In 2002, the story of Salvation Mountain was even entered into the U.S. Congressional Record, with the site being described as a "national treasure."[2]

The first time my family visited Salvation Mountain, Leonard was just beginning to build little sections on the side of the mountain using bales of hay, tree branches, and other odd pieces of "junk" he found in the desert. Ultimately, he was able to accomplish his vision of bringing the message of God's love to many people. The delightfully colored Salvation Mountain is still being visited by thousands of tourists who have heard about it through social media, the Internet, and word of mouth. The entire story is fascinating, and the mountain has become a must-see attraction for anyone interested in experiencing an unusual day out in the desert!

---

2. "Leonard Knight and Salvation Mountain," 107th Cong., 2nd sess., *Congressional Record* 148 (May 15, 2002): S4383–84, https://www.congress.gov/crec/2002/05/15/CREC-2002-05-15-pt1-PgS4383-3.pdf.

Leonard passed on to his heavenly reward in 2014. Since that time, Salvation Mountain has been cared for by a group of supporters, and it is maintained through the generous donations of those who visit the site.[3] Leonard's testimony of perseverance is a reminder that God's purposes will be fulfilled in our lives if we remain yielded to the Spirit and stay connected in love to Him and others. Creative glory will find a way![4]

YIELDING TO THE PROCESS

The patriarch Job spoke in artistic terms about the process of testing we endure during the trials of life: *"But He knows the way that I take [and He pays attention to it]. When He has tried me, I will come forth as [refined] gold [pure and luminous]"* (Job 23:10 AMP). Through creative glory, we are given the opportunity to advance by the Spirit even in the midst of great difficulty. If we stay on track with God, we will ultimately come out better at the end than when we first began. The key is to stay focused on God and remain faithful to Him.

Your life itself is a work of art in progress. It would be wrong to look at a painting or a sculpture in the middle of its creation and judge it before it was finalized. Yet, so many times, we criticize ourselves while God is still working on us. (See, for example, 1 Thessalonians 5:23–24.) According to the Psalms, God is the Master Potter, and we are the clay:

> And yet, O LORD, you are our Father. We are the clay, and you are the potter. We all are formed by your hand. (Isaiah 64:8 NLT)

In the natural world, clay doesn't offer resistance to a potter. Similarly, we need to surrender to God's loving and careful touch. He takes pleasure in molding, transforming, and sanctifying us as we journey through this earthly life. We must learn how to yield ourselves to the guiding hands of our Creator. When we yield to Him, we become the masterpiece He desires to display to the world around us.

YOUR LIFE ITSELF IS A WORK OF ART IN PROGRESS.

---

3. For more information about Salvation Mountain, visit www.salvationmountain.us.
4. The photo on the back cover of this book and the photos on the chapter start pages were taken at Salvation Mountain. Please see copyright page for photo credit.

EXPRESSING THE HEAVENLY VISION

I first met Akiane Kramarik when she was about twelve. I had been ministering in Coeur d'Alene, Idaho, and she frequented the church that hosted me. After one of the meetings, Akiane invited me to her home to see some of her paintings. I expected to see childlike paintings, but what I saw amazed me. Wall after wall in her home was covered with stunning, lifelike paintings of Jesus.

Akiane told me that both her mother and father were atheists, so she grew up in an unbelieving atmosphere. But at the tender age of four, she was taken into a heavenly vision and had an encounter with the Lord Jesus. While Akiane was lifted up to the heavenlies in this way, the Lord put a pencil in her hand and told her to draw.

After this encounter, she picked up a pencil and a pad of paper, and she began to draw. What she drew surprised everyone, including Akiane. When her mother saw the picture, she couldn't believe her daughter had created such a drawing. "Show me," her mother insisted, and she stood over her child while Akiane drew another picture, which was as good as the first one.

"How did you do that? How did you make this?" her mother asked. The questions were legitimate. Akiane had absolutely no professional training, and yet she was suddenly producing remarkable images. She told her mother what had happened to her.

Akiane had other visions, and, a couple of years later, she was taken into a heavenly vision in which the Lord handed her a paintbrush and said, "I want you to paint." When she returned to her room, she picked up a paintbrush and began painting breathtaking images of what she had seen in her vision—the Lord Jesus Christ.

Akiane got in the habit of waking up very early in the morning, going to the basement of her home, and painting when no one was watching. She painted what God was showing her in visions. A I mentioned earlier, the images she painted of Jesus are extremely realistic, and each painting seems to have a glow about it. Many people who have viewed these paintings have had encounters of their own with the Lord, all because of the special anointing upon Akiane's art.

While I was with Akiane in her home that day, she took me to her bedroom and showed me a small keyboard. Then she said, "I heard you say that the Lord taught you how to play the piano. I want to learn to play the piano too." I laid my hands on her and prayed for her and blessed her. Soon after I left, she sat down and began playing her little piano.

Today, Akiane is talented in both the visual and musical arts (and she also writes poetry). She creates with remarkable depth. She can paint beautifully and play skillfully, yet she still has had no professional training. To me, she is an example of what God wants to do for His people through creative glory.[5]

A CLOUD OF GLORY

While I was writing my book *Power Portals*, I reached out to my friend John Almaguer in Ashville, North Carolina, who creates glass artwork that represents and reflects the glory of God. Many years earlier, John had given me one of his beautiful pieces that represents a heavenly portal, and I wanted to send additional "glass portals" to some friends, along with a copy of the new book. I have kept that special portal piece on my bookshelf over the years, and whenever I see it, it reminds me of the open heavens that Christ has made accessible for us through Himself. Anointed artwork can help us to remember God's promises and minister deeply to our hearts. Many of the friends to whom I sent a glass portal sculpture wrote and thanked me, saying that it had become a daily reminder for them of the power of praise, prayer, and open heavens.

John's relationship with the heavenly Father is demonstrated through his creativity. He states on his website, "Creating something that has never been seen before excites me. I make unseen things come alive in the manifest realm. What a joy to dance this dance of creating works that God dreamt of making through me long before I even breathed. And now I breathe, and art is formed."[6]

Another friend of mine, Jasalyn Thorne, is an artist and award-winning photographer in Vancouver, British Columbia. Her work has been featured in

---

5. To learn more about Akiane Kramarik, see "About Akiane," Akiane Gallery, https://akiane.com/about/.
6. John Almaguer, "Artist Statement," http://www.almaguerglass.com/p/about.html.

publications like *Vogue, Elle, Hello Canada*, and *Fashion* magazine.[7] Janet and I first met Jasalyn while we were living in Western Canada. Last year, I noticed on social media that Jasalyn was painting beautiful swirls of all shapes, sizes, and colors. She said that, initially, she didn't know exactly what she was painting but felt a strong leading to continue creating in this unusual way.

When I first saw these swirls, I immediately knew in my spirit what Jasalyn was painting. They were power portals: red, blue, gold, black, white, and purple ones. They were prophetically opening through her artwork with every color and promise imaginable. Jasalyn began to realize this too. Her unique paintings were creative demonstrations of spiritual portals opening within her. This Holy Spirit-directed art carries the essence of creative glory. I was struck by the powerful anointing that rested upon these paintings, so we commissioned Jasalyn to paint a golden portal for the cover artwork of our soaking and prayer album *Opening the Portals*. We now have this original painting hanging in the front entrance of our home, welcoming all our guests to the glory realm.

Through creative gifts, God blesses, encourages, ministers healing, and even imparts anointings to people. We do not and should not build shrines or create idolatrous images that bring attention only to themselves. However, we *are* called to build a cloud of glory through the arts with the God-given gifts He offers us. We know from the Scriptures that what the Spirit leads us to create can also be anointed by the Spirit. (See Exodus 40:9.) Open spiritual doorways through the arts become bridges for others to connect with the Lord of all so they can see Him and know Him.

POWER PORTALS OF CREATIVITY

Although God can pour out His creative glory upon us wherever we are, I have found that there are some places on earth where I feel closer and more connected to the Lord. Many people have experienced the same reality. For example, my wife, Janet, loves going to the beach. Her idea of an ideal vacation would be our spending a week in Hawaii, sitting by the pool or on the sandy shores, watching the aquamarine waves of the Pacific Ocean roll in and out as we are bathed in warm sunlight. Beyond enjoying the natural beauty of the

7. "About Jasalyn," Jasalyn Thorne Photography, https://jasalynthornephotography.com/info.

Hawaiian Islands, Janet just feels at peace there. Many times, she has spoken to me about the way she feels wrapped in the *aloha* (love and breath) of God when she is on Hawaiian land. She senses a spiritual connection—a power portal— that specially communicates God's beauty and enwraps her heart in His love.

I encourage you to find specific places that inspire you, too—places that stir up your creativity, places that energize you. Have you found your creative space? A place where you can connect to the glory realm unhindered by earthly distractions?

Of course, we know that God is everywhere, but we must also understand that places are important to Him, and He has created a specific, secret place for each and every one of us where we can retreat into holy connection with our Creator. You will recognize your special place when you find it. You might even say that you "resonate" with that certain location.

The divine energy in a power portal acts like an amplifier. An amplifier is defined as "an electronic device (as in a stereo system) for amplifying voltage, current, or power."[8] In other words, an amplifier takes a signal and makes it stronger. When we are in a power portal, the manifest presence of God will amplify whatever we bring to it—whether it is spiritual, mental, or physical. I've noticed that when I step into a portal, I am strengthened spiritually; I am filled with new confidence regarding God's love for me and others. Divine wisdom and personal revelation are profoundly present, along with every other provision that is needed in that moment. In this realm, my thoughts also suddenly become clearer, inspirational ideas flow like a river, and I am flooded with heightened feelings of peace, joy, and heavenly security. In a power portal, creative glory comes alive! In addition, I feel physically buoyant. When we step into a power portal, we feel healthy and alive—more vibrantly alive than we've ever felt before! There is no pain, discomfort, or sense of sickness in an open portal.

There is a particular location I like to go to that I often refer to as "The Portal." It has been my own personal secret place on many occasions. When I was ready to write my book *Power Portals*, I went to this portal with a pad of paper and a pen, found a nice rock to sit on, and began writing. This location is within an almost two-mile loop trail through a steep and rugged terrain of

---

8. *Merriam-Webster.com Dictionary*, s.v. "amplifier," https://www.merriam-webster.com/dictionary/amplifier.

cactus, smoke trees, other native plants, and wildlife. The ultimate reward of trekking up and down those rocky steps is that it leads to the breathtaking waterfall at the base of the San Jacinto mountains that I mentioned at the beginning of chapter 1. The melting winter snow running down the side of the mountain provides the purest (and possibly coldest) pool of water that I've ever swum in. Yes, it's very cold, but it's also very glorious! There's just something about that place that puts my mind and spirit into a proper position to hear and connect with the Spirit.

Recently, a minister friend of mine reached out to me, asking for directions to the portal. He was feeling discouraged and just needed some prayerful time alone with the Lord. After spending a couple of days at the portal, he contacted me and said, "I had three angelic encounters there!" The experience was life-shifting for him because the Lord reaffirmed his call and reassured him of His providence.

I wasn't surprised to hear that he had encountered angels at the portal. Angels are always present wherever God's glory resides. When I visit this particular portal, I often see a tall angel standing in the center of the waterfall wearing a rainbow halo around his head like a band. Sometimes the rainbow is fitted around his waist like a belt. In the tenth chapter of Revelation, the Bible speaks about an angel with a rainbow halo, and his predominant message is this: "There will be no more delay." (See Revelation 10:1–7.) The angel that stands in the portal seems to work to encourage the acceleration of God's purposes in the earth. That is the testimony many people have shared after visiting this special place.

I remember the first time we led a group of people down to this portal. The Spirit was moving in such a special way that many people asked if I would be willing to baptize them in the pool at the base of the waterfall. Their desire to fully commit their lives to Christ was accelerated in the portal. Although we hadn't prepared for a service of water baptism, we made room for what God wanted to do. When creative glory comes on the scene, be prepared to flow in the spontaneity of the moment.

CREATIVE GLORY IS RISING UP

As we have seen, God desires to use His people to put His glory on display. Divine expressions of glory manifest when we give creative glory room to flow—in any sphere of society. If there's one place where creative worship should always be accepted, it should certainly be in God's house, His church. Again, there are no limitations in the realm of creative glory. However, for far too long, the church has tried to separate the arts from spirituality. There can be no separation between the two. As we discussed in chapter 1, God is the essence of pure creativity, and creative glory flows from Him. God can use the arts to bring people closer to Himself and to receive salvation in Christ.

I clearly remember when "worship flags" were first being introduced to the body of Christ at large, and their use was controversial. Some people didn't feel comfortable incorporating a different style of worship, and church boardrooms and church leadership meetings around the world were filled with discussions about whether or not flags and banners should be used during worship services.

The same type of issue arose regarding the use of drums and other modern musical instruments in church. Could the Lord receive glory from the use of these instruments, which were, in the minds of many, associated with worldly music? There were similar disagreements concerning dancing. When I was a young child, the Christians I knew never danced. We all had preconceived ideas about what dancing was, and, in general, dancing was frowned upon. We never went to dances, we never danced to music at home, and we certainly never danced in church. We were under the impression that dancing was a worldly act, and it only belonged with those who were secular.

I was about ten when I saw people dancing in church for the very first time. I was visiting my grandparents' church, and what impressed me about the believers there was how much freedom they had and how joyful they were when they danced! They seemed to be so happy celebrating the goodness of God! I remember how delighted I felt in that atmosphere and how I wished that people in our church would dance like that too! My heart was open to the possibility that God could do something in our worship services that we had not previously accepted.

Not long after that experience, one Sunday, I was praising the Lord with the other members of my home congregation when, suddenly, a joyous exuberance came over everyone, and people began dancing before the Lord for the very first time! I'll never forget it because I began to dance too! It seemed like my little feet were moving a million miles a minute, shuffling back and forth, bouncing my little body up and down as I praised the Lord! I was dancing in the Spirit, and I felt so much freedom and so much joy!

After that service, we no longer struggled with the issue of dancing in church. Creative glory had moved into the sanctuary and made clear to us that dancing in the Spirit was not only acceptable but was also to be welcomed. We could now understand and come into agreement with the following passage of Scripture:

> David was dancing before the LORD with great enthusiasm…. So David and all the house of Israel were bringing the ark of the LORD up [to the City of David] with shouts [of joy] and with the sound of the trumpet.
>
> (2 Samuel 6:14–15 AMP)

Have you opened your heart to all the possibilities of creative glory? God desires to do so much more in your life than you've previously permitted Him to do. But you must be willing to allow Him to move past your head and into your heart. Permit God to do a creative work in your heart, and when He does, your head will receive it too.

Let us give God praise through *all* of the arts. There are unlimited realms of creative glory.

Let the flaggers flag!

Let the musicians play!

Let the dancers dance!

Let the Lord receive His glory!

Creative glory is rising up!

CREATIVITY AND SENSITIVITY

Several years ago, Janet and I had the opportunity to tour the magnificent Sistine Chapel in Vatican City, Rome. Michelangelo's masterwork was breathtaking, to say the least. And I couldn't even begin to count the number of angels and holy scenes depicted in all the paintings, murals, and sculptures on display throughout Rome. It is much the same in a number of European cities. Creative expression helps us to connect with higher spiritual realities.

It seems to me that those who are more in touch with their creative side generally tend to be more in touch with the spiritual world as well. Or maybe it's the other way around: those who are spiritual are creative. Whichever way you look at it, throughout the centuries, countless artists have painted beautiful masterpieces featuring God, Jesus, and the angels.

On the flip side, some of the most tormented people I know are artists. This may be because—knowingly or unknowingly—they have used the doorways of their imaginations to open demonic portals into dark places. We must guard our imaginations and protect the seer gift that's been given to us. The same imagination that opens our eyes to God's unseen realm can also open our eyes to ungodly, destructive elements if we are not careful.

As a young child, I was exposed to pornography on several occasions. Although it was a very long time ago, I still remember the first time it happened. We lived on the very outskirts of the city, and there was a large farmer's field beside our home. My brother and I often liked playing in that field with the other neighborhood kids, making mazes or building forts amid the cornstalks that grew high at the end of summer. One day, those mazes led us into an open clearing in the middle of the field. In the center of that clearing was an old tractor tire, and inside that tire were handfuls of dirty magazines.

What we discovered that day was perverted and inappropriate for us to look at. Although I had never previously known that this type of material existed, in my heart, I knew that it was wrong for us to view those dirty images. My conscience and the voice of the Spirit told me so. I call them "dirty" because that's exactly how they made me feel.

Soon after that, my brother and I were playing at a neighbor's house, and one of the boys invited us into his parents' bedroom to see his father's "special collection." Just walking into that room, I felt an uneasiness in my stomach. I should have retreated at that moment, but, instead, I followed the others all the way inside, only to find stacks and stacks of dirty magazines. They filled the drawers and were piled underneath the bed. Everywhere you looked in that bedroom were images of people performing all types of inappropriate acts.

My brother and I went back home and told our parents what had happened and what we had seen, and they told us never to go back to that home. However, those images left impressions on my soul. To this day, the images sometimes arise on the screen of my mind; when this happens, I must take authority over them, casting down those vain imaginations. (See 2 Corinthians 10:5.) One of the ways the enemy attempts to steal people's innocence and purity is through such experiences. Whether you're consciously aware of it or not, what you see will leave a lasting impression on your soul.

This applies to both what is pure and what is unholy. That is why it's necessary for you to do a personal inventory each time you sit down to watch a movie or television show, play a video game, look at something on the Internet, or even read a book. What you see matters. And it is much easier to avoid ungodly images and ideas than to try to "un-see" or "un-remember" them once they've been burned into the sensitive fiber of your imagination.

Guard your eyes. Protect them. They are the door to your soul. As a creative person, you have the God-given desire to see new things, explore new possibilities, and go beyond the limits of what's been done before. The enemy knows that, too, and he wants to exploit this inclination. Therefore, you must pay close attention to God's voice, which safely leads you and guards you against the enemy's assaults.

If you have been struggling in this area, or if you have experienced trauma due to having been exposed to explicit images, I want you to know that you're not alone and that God can cleanse you. Please pray with me now to receive release, freedom, and protection:

> Father, in the name of Jesus, I thank You for washing my mind with the cleansing power of the blood of Christ. I plead the blood over my imagination and creativity. Right now, I give You every vain idea, imagination, and image that the enemy has attempted to place within my creative soul. I release these to You now, and I know that You bring me the freedom to create with purity and holiness as I seek You and Your ways. Amen!

It is essential to guard the portal of your eyes (as well as the portals of all your other senses) from evil so you can create all that God has planned for you to create. We need creative glory now more than ever before. The redeemed creative arts are vital to opening new dimensions for those who are willing to take a look into heavenly realms. What you see in the supernatural, you can create in the natural. Painting can become an open window for others to experience heaven. Musical notes can become an invitation into the realm of healing. Writing can unlock doors for discovering new places in God. Whatever your gift, many people are waiting to see what you have seen in the Spirit.

WHAT YOU SEE IN THE SUPERNATURAL,
YOU CAN CREATE IN THE NATURAL.

CHANGED BY CREATIVE GLORY

In the early days of our ministry, I met a powerful couple, Rev. Edgar and Holly Baillie, near Rockford, Illinois. The Baillies had a great miracle ministry, and that ministry greatly impacted my life. Edgar has since "crossed the river," but, to this day, Holly continues ministering in the power of the Spirit as God opens doors of connection for her. As I was developing this book, the Spirit reminded me of a testimony Edgar had personally shared with me many years ago. I asked Holly for permission to include it in *Creative Glory*, and she graciously obliged. It is a beautiful testimony of Edgar's salvation and how creative glory opened to him in a moment of deep desperation. I share this testimony with you in Edgar's own words:

I was having trouble with a business deal, and it was serious. I knew that if I did not come up with a large amount of money, it would cause problems for my business and my family. I saw no way out, so I decided to take my life.

I went and found my old police revolver. I had been a policeman in Colton, California, some years earlier and had always kept my revolver. I took my gun and started up the stairs to end my life. As I walked up the stairs, something caught my eye from the wall beside me. There was a beautiful painting of the San Luis Rey mission in California, a picture that my daughter P.J. had painted. At the top of the mission was a cross, and this cross seemed like it was glowing, something it had never done and could not do! I looked at it to see what the glow was, and the cross seemed to glow even more brightly.

Although I didn't understand what was happening, I now recognize that a supernatural manifestation was taking place in that painting! In the very next moment, I heard a mysterious voice say, "Edgar, go into the church." The next thing I knew, I was standing there, looking down at my body, which was lying facedown on the stairs! I went into the painting, into the church, and there I came face-to-face with the glory of Jesus Christ Himself.

He was more real than anyone or anything on this earth, more real than anything I had ever encountered! He said to me, "Edgar, go back! I have a great and mighty work for you to do!"

I said, "How, Lord? How do I get back into my body?"

He said, "*Think* your way in."

I went back into my body and came alive for the first time in my life! I ran through the house, jumping over furniture and screaming, "He's real! He's really REAL!" My first wife, Charlotte (who passed away many years ago now), was a born-again believer, and she had been praying for me to meet Jesus for fifteen years. I had never known or understood that Jesus Christ was really real until that moment.

Now I knew I had to go find Charlotte and tell her! She was working at a grocery store, and we had agreed that I would pick her up for lunch, so I jumped in the car to go find her. When she opened the door to get in the car, she took one look at me and said, "What happened to you?" She could see, by just looking at me, that I was not the same man she had been married to all those years. I had been changed by the glory of Jesus!

Creative glory will change you. Creative glory will encourage you. Creative glory will inspire you. Creative glory will open new doors for you. I pray that you will embrace the realm of creative glory flowing into your life. As you do, divine expression will be released through you!

CREATIVE GLORY! LET THIS GLORY ARISE IN ME!

THE CREATIVE MIND

*"By faith [that is, with an inherent trust and enduring confidence
in the power, wisdom and goodness of God] we understand that the
worlds (universe, ages) were framed and created [formed, put in order,
and equipped for their intended purpose] by the word of God, so that
what is seen was not made out of things which are visible."*
—Hebrews 11:3 (AMP)

God created *everything* in the universe. Yet the Word says, *"What is seen
was not made out of things which are visible."* From what did God make the
universe? He made it from the same source from which He made you—His
mind.

Humankind is God's brilliant idea. He didn't create you out of "things."
You are, in reality, the very manifestation of His imagination. Speaking to
the prophet Jeremiah, the Spirit said:

*Before I formed you in the womb I knew you [and approved of you as
My chosen instrument], and before you were born I consecrated you*

[to Myself as My own]; I have appointed you as a prophet to the nations.
(Jeremiah 1:5 AMP)

God knew Jeremiah before the prophet was even formed in the womb. The same is true of you and me. God knew us before we were flesh and blood. This is an awesome thought! Again, how could God know us before we came into the world? He knew us in His mind, and He created us out of His heart.

Out of His divine imagination, God created everything that exists. And it is out of your redeemed imagination, as you follow the leading of the Spirit in the glory realm, that you can create things too. The redeemed imagination is one that is able to see God, understand His ways, and envision divine expressions that bring glory to the Creator.

Since God cannot be seen by the physical eyes of mankind, we might think, "God is completely invisible." However, while He may be invisible in our three-dimensional world, He can make Himself as visible to us as He wants to. Why? Because He is really *not* invisible. He can be seen. The Bible indicates that the angels can see Him. The living creatures can see Him. The heavenly elders can see Him. The cherubim and seraphim can see Him. (See, for example, Revelation 4.) So, the truth is that God is not invisible; He can be seen with spiritual eyes. And He can also be "seen" by mankind's perception and imagination. If He can be seen in these ways, then He is not all-inclusively invisible.

Hebrews 11:6 says, "*Without faith it is impossible to [walk with God and] please Him*" (AMP). While you are on this earth, you need to see God with your faith, with your confident belief. Jesus said to Thomas, "*Because you have seen Me, do you now believe? Blessed [happy, spiritually secure, and favored by God] are they who did not see [Me] and yet believed [in Me]*" (John 20:29 AMP). This is exactly what God is expecting from you today. He wants you to believe in Him with your heart, with your mind, with your inner being. I call such belief the "imagination," using the term *imagination* in a broader way than it is usually used. It does not only refer to what we create in our own minds but also to what we dwell on and conceive of based on the reality of God and the spiritual realm.

RENEWING YOUR MIND

To see God with our imaginations, our minds need to be sanctified and renewed. Writing to the Romans, Paul said:

And do not be conformed to this world [any longer with its superficial values and customs], but be transformed and progressively changed [as you mature spiritually] by the renewing of your mind [focusing on godly values and ethical attitudes], so that you may prove [for yourselves] what the will of God is, that which is good and acceptable and perfect [in His plan and purpose for you]. (Romans 12:2 AMP)

God wants you to be transformed completely—body, soul, and spirit. He desires to touch the inward part of you that is able to dream, imagine, and receive ideas from the creative-glory realm. He wants to renew your mind with His thoughts. And as you meditate upon His ways and His Word, He will transform you.

Isaiah declared:

You will keep in perfect and constant peace the one whose mind is steadfast [that is, committed and focused on You—in both inclination and character], because he trusts and takes refuge in You [with hope and confident expectation]. (Isaiah 26:3 AMP)

God will keep you *"in perfect and constant peace"* while launching you into realms in which you begin to declare and release heaven here on earth. How can this happen? It can only happen as your mind is sanctified—meaning set apart and consecrated as holy—as your imagination is focused on Him, as you trust in Him, and as you receive the Word of God into your inner being and let it be manifested through you.

There is a process that the Bible calls *"the washing with water through the word"* (Ephesians 5:26 NIV). Have you allowed God to wash you by the water of His Word as you read, meditate on, memorize, and study the Scriptures? Such washing renews your mind, and you are transformed by it. You begin thinking God's thoughts, dreaming God's dreams, and seeing God's visions. Your heart is set ablaze with God's revelations, and your imagination comes alive.

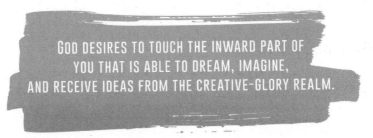

GOD DESIRES TO TOUCH THE INWARD PART OF YOU THAT IS ABLE TO DREAM, IMAGINE, AND RECEIVE IDEAS FROM THE CREATIVE-GLORY REALM.

RISING TO A HIGHER STANDARD

You and I have a choice to make. We can allow our thoughts to be conformed to this world, or we can rise to a higher standard. God has declared:

As the heavens are higher than the earth, so my ways are higher than your ways and my thoughts higher than your thoughts. (Isaiah 55:9 NLT)

If you want, you can remain tied to your own thinking and understanding; you can stay confined within your limited, natural way of living. But if that is your choice, you will never move into the greater things God has for you. Creative glory is broad, expansive, and overflowing with supernatural opportunities. God's thoughts are higher than our thoughts, and His ways are higher than our ways. Let Him wash you with His Word. Let Him transform you by renewing your mind. Let Him touch the realm of your thoughts, your imagination, with His creative glory.

Jesus was a gifted storyteller who captivated people's imaginations with His anointed words. When He spoke, miracles appeared on the scene and other extraordinary things happened. His words were powerful because they were *true*. He was not entertaining people's fleshly desires. He was challenging their hearts and minds.

Today, God wants to do and say things through His people that will captivate millions and draw them to Himself and His glory. He doesn't just want to entertain us; He wants to engage our imaginations and open them to the Technicolor presence of creative glory. Why? Because, as Proverbs 29:18 declares, "*Where there is no vision [no revelation of God and His word], the people are unrestrained; but happy and blessed is he who keeps the law [of God]*" (AMP). Another translation says, "*Where there is no vision, the people perish*" (KJVER). In the church, creating programs and participating in activities are not enough. There must be heavenly vision. There may be a lot going on in your church, but is there vision—revelation—from God? Or are people in your church perishing for lack of vision? Without an understanding of God's imagination, people will perish in various ways. But when they have vision from God, people will prosper in His limitless ability. God wants to download the imagination of heaven to His church here on earth. Let the Spirit reveal His thoughts to you. Let Him connect with your spirit and unfold to you the realms of creative glory.

John wrote to the first-century church:

Beloved, I pray that in every way you may succeed and prosper and be in good health [physically], just as [I know] your soul prospers [spiritually].
(3 John 1:2 AMP)

We can only succeed and prosper as our souls, or our imaginations, succeed and prosper. To do this, they must connect with God's glory. There is an abundance of good things awaiting us in creative glory. Paul encouraged the early church with these words: *"And my God will liberally supply (fill until full) your every need according to His riches in glory in Christ Jesus"* (Philippians 4:19 AMP). How will God liberally supply all our needs? Not according to the limited resources of the earth and not according to our individual financial wealth. He will do it *"according to His riches in glory in Christ Jesus."* God will reveal these *"riches"* to us through heavenly visions, glory visions, in living color. We just need to be open to them. I believe this is the reason the following phrase is repeated so many times in the book of Revelation:

He who has an ear, let him hear and heed what the Spirit says to the churches.　　(Revelation 2:7 AMP; see also 2:11, 17, 29; 3:6, 13, 22)

Are you hearing and heeding what the Spirit is saying to you today?

> CREATIVE GLORY IS BROAD, EXPANSIVE, AND OVERFLOWING WITH SUPERNATURAL OPPORTUNITIES.

SPEAKING WHAT GOD SHOWS YOU

God might say something to me, but unless I am open to hear and heed it, it will not benefit me. I must have a mind that is willing to perceive, and then receive, a heavenly vision. I also have to be willing to speak that vision forth—to declare it and move into the reality of it. It is at that point—when I have believed God's thoughts and begun speaking them—that His thoughts become enthroned in my vocabulary. I speak what He is speaking, and therefore my vocabulary contains His vision.

Let's return to the first two verses of Genesis, which is the book of beginnings:

In the beginning God created the heavens and the earth. The earth was formless and empty, and darkness covered the deep waters. And the Spirit of God was hovering over the surface of the waters. (Genesis 1:1–2 NLT)

God's Spirit was "*hovering*" over the waters. His presence was there. His glory was there. His ability was there. Still, creation had not yet come forth. In order to bring forth creation, God did something else: He *spoke* creation into existence. "*Then God said, 'Let there be light,' and there was light*" (Genesis 1:3 NLT, NKJV). It was when His thoughts came forth clothed in the vocabulary of His words that His imagination became physical manifestation.

Again, God wants to capture the attention of your mind, your imagination, and your thoughts with His revelation. When that happens, great things can be accomplished as you speak His will into existence on earth. When you begin to proclaim what the Lord has shown you—declaring the purposes of God, the ability of God, the imagination of God—then what you are speaking will begin to surround you in outstanding ways. The connections you need will come. The provisions you need will come. The opportunities you need will come.

Although God reveals Himself to us and teaches us through His Word, many times, He also communicates with us directly through our thoughts. As He foretold through the prophet Joel:

I will pour out my Spirit upon all people. Your sons and daughters will prophesy. Your old men will dream dreams, and your young men will see visions. (Joel 2:28 NLT)

Many people make the mistake of deciding to put on the back burner something God has spoken to them. Because they "are not sure" it was from God, they choose not to say anything or do anything about it. They don't even bother to write it down. Then they wonder why they're not prospering in their lives. It is not your own vision that will cause you to prosper; it is heaven's vision that will cause you to rise up in a greater way. So, when you think you may have received a word from God, instead of putting it on the back burner, begin to pray about it, seek wise counsel, and then move forward in faith as that word is confirmed. God wants to give you revelation through creative glory. He wants to give you a vision of who He is. He wants to manifest *His* thoughts through *your* thoughts, words, and actions. Throughout the history of the world, God has always chosen men and women to speak and act for Him on earth, and He continues to choose men and women to speak and act for Him. Today, He has chosen you!

What is the result of the Spirit being poured out upon God's people? They receive prophecy, dreams, and visions—all of which relate to the imagination of man. These revelations are downloaded to us from the Spirit of creative glory. Joel 2:30 (NLT, AMP) speaks of *"wonders,"* *"blood and fire"* and *"columns of smoke."* Believing and declaring God's vision causes supernatural occurrences in the natural world around us.

BEING CAPTIVATED BY OUR CREATOR

Jesus Christ is the King of all kings and the Lord of all lords. He is the Creator of all creators. He is the Designer of all designers. He is the Painter of all painters. He is the Sculptor of all sculptors. He is the Animator of all animators. He is the Singer of all singers. He is the Dancer of all dancers. He is the Author of all authors. He is the Engineer of all engineers. He is the Inventor of all inventors. He is the Originator of all expressions of true creativity—and, by His divine presence, He wants to captivate your mind and emotions; He wants to give you fresh expressions of His mind and heart to communicate to the world.

In the past, you may have been entertained by social media, television, movies, radio, or music. These things may have their place in our lives, but this is the day to be "entertained" by the Entertainer of all entertainers. God wants to entertain your soul with His creative glory.

Some years ago, Janet and I were invited by Pastor Yong Jo Ha, the founder of Onnuri Community Church in Seoul, Korea, to participate in a great soul-winning event in the Saitama Super Arena near Tokyo. Tens of thousands of people were gathered in the stadium. Because there were so many great ministries in attendance, I was given a slot of fifteen minutes to minister during an afternoon service. I praised and worshipped God and prophesied, and as I did, the glory began falling all over the stadium. Gold fillings and gold teeth began appearing in the mouths of people who had dental issues. Creative miracles of all kinds began happening, along with unusual signs and wonders. As God was doing these miracles, the men and women who were the entertainers for this event—actors and actresses from a much-loved Asian soap opera—were in their dressing rooms, rehearsing and getting ready for their performance. They saw by telecast what was happening in the main stadium and began to feel the Spirit of Glory and be touched by Him.

After our fifteen-minute session was over, Janet and I were on our way back up to our sky box to watch the rest of the meeting when one of the managers of those performers came to us and asked, "Would you come and pray for the actors and actresses? We have never, ever seen them touched in this way before." We agreed to go down to their dressing rooms to pray for them and minister to them. As we ministered, God gave me a prophetic word that He was going to use these performers with an anointing such as they had experienced that day—not just in their workplace, but also in their personal lives. As they entertained people, a supernatural anointing would flow through them to touch others with the creative glory of God.

As I spoke this prophetic word, many of the performers began to weep. Afterward, some of them came to Janet and me and said they'd always had the idea that they had a secular job in entertainment and that their walk with the Lord was to be totally separate from it. They were Christians, but they didn't live like true believers in their profession. When they went to work, they changed clothes and put on the "masks" of entertainers. God was saying that He wanted to use them as entertainers, but He also wanted them to be *anointed* entertainers. He desired that they live as true believers at all times so that His creative glory would rest upon them in every aspect of their lives, in every way, everywhere they went.

They wept as they said, "You could not have known it, but that was what was in our hearts. We have been praying and asking the Spirit for that. Still, we were not sure it could ever happen because the church has very strict classifications for those who are in ministry and those who are not. What is done inside the church is considered sacred, and what is done outside the church is considered secular."

How sad! That is such a mistaken concept. If you are a believer in Jesus, wherever you go, you are a minister of His glorious gospel. God promises that He will give you every place that your feet touch for the kingdom. (See, for example, Joshua 1:3.) God wants to use you, letting His glory flow through you wherever you are. A. W. Tozer said, "The Holy Spirit never enters a man and then lets him live like the world."[9] The Spirit desires to fill your mind with His thoughts, His ideas, His dreams so that you might be a more effective witness among all the people you meet and in all the places you go as you live for Him.

This, of course, includes whatever you do on a daily basis. Jesus is our example in this regard. He was 100 percent effective in His ministry because He only said what He heard the Father saying, and He only did what He saw the Father doing. (See John 5:19; 12:49.) How did Jesus know what the Father was saying and doing? He knew it because His mind was filled with creative glory.

God is not just looking for "a few good people." He is looking for thousands, even millions, of people who are willing to have their minds entertained by heaven. These are men, women, boys, and girls who have their minds stayed on God at all times, in all seasons, no matter what they are going through. They understand heavenly purpose. If you will determine to keep your mind on heavenly things (see Colossians 3:1–3), to believe God's truth and act on it, there is no limit to what He can do through you.

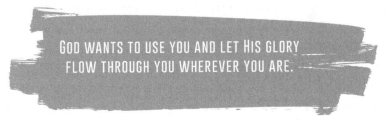

GOD WANTS TO USE YOU AND LET HIS GLORY FLOW THROUGH YOU WHEREVER YOU ARE.

LIVING ACCORDING TO THE TRUTH

Whatever God says is true, and whatever the enemy says is a lie—whether it is an outright lie, a half-truth, or a twisted truth. If you determine to live according to the Word of truth, and not according to false ideas and beliefs, then whatever lies the enemy says about you cannot come to pass. What is a believer? It is someone who believes the truth. Sadly, many people have been believing what the enemy has said about them, and their lives reflect it. God

9. A. W. Tozer, *The Quotable Tozer*, ed. James L. Snyder (Bloomington, MN: Bethany House Publishers, 2018), 170.

is calling you to reject the enemy's lies and to receive what He says. He wants to fill your mind with His eternal truth.

Janet and I were in Hollywood some years ago, and God gave us a divine appointment. We've had many opportunities to minister on set with people in the entertainment industry, and the Spirit has always surprised us by the ways in which He has moved among those who were seeking the truth. In this instance, we ended up on the set of *Desperate Housewives*. I turned to Janet and said, "They don't even know what they're so desperate for." I believe God wants to fill even the soap operas with His glory. Instead of depicting people breaking up, they will portray people getting back together. Instead of showing people cursing at one another, they will depict people blessing one another. I can see it now: *As the World Turns*, *All My Children*, led by the *Guiding Light*, will no longer be *The Young and the Restless*; instead, they will be *The Bold and the Beautiful*; no longer will they be on *The Edge of Night* or in the *General Hospital*, but they will be in *Another World* filled with glory all the *Days of Our Lives*. Hallelujah!

ACCESSING THE GLORY REALM

We don't yet know all that God wants to do through our redeemed minds in the glory realm (see, for example, Ephesians 3:20), but I have had spiritual experiences that have given me glimpses of it. Many years ago, Janet and I planned a trip from Canada to the United States to establish U.S. ministry offices in Southern California. As we were about to leave, at the last minute, I realized that I didn't have my wedding band, my pinky ring, and my watch, all of which I usually wore in public. I looked all over the house for them but couldn't find them. I asked Janet and Lincoln to help me, but they couldn't find them either. I called our ministry office and asked our office administrator to look around for them there, but she, too, was unable to locate them. In the end, Janet, Lincoln, and I had to leave Canada without them. It just so happened that the week we were in California was our wedding anniversary, and I felt terrible about not having my wedding band to wear. Janet and I went out to celebrate on the night of our anniversary, and we had a good time; however, throughout the evening, I felt terrible about not being able to wear my wedding band.

The next night, we planned to go out again. Before we left, I was sitting in an easy chair, Janet was preparing for the evening, and Lincoln was watching a cartoon on television. I decided to lie back in the chair and take a rest while I waited. Immediately, I fell asleep and started dreaming. I don't usually remember my dreams unless God speaks to me specifically through them. However, I'm believing that God will increase the particular type of dream I had that day.

In this dream, I was in our offices in Canada, and I received a word of knowledge that the rings and the watch I was looking for were right there in the office mailbox. I immediately went to look in the mailbox, and, just as the Spirit had shown me, there were the two rings and the watch. One by one, I took them out and put them on.

I was in a very deep sleep, but suddenly the sound from the television in the room seemed to blare. Some character in the cartoon was screaming. Startled, I woke up, looked at Lincoln, and said, "Lincoln, turn down the TV." As I said that, I caught sight of my hand, and I saw that I was now wearing my wedding band, my pinky ring, and my watch!

I was in California, and my rings and watch had been left in Canada. In the natural, I hadn't gone anywhere. I had just been sitting in my chair. But I'd had a dream, and in that dream, God invaded my imagination. He entertained my mind with creative glory. Supernatural dreams are doorways into the glory realm, and a door had opened for me. In the dream, God had given me a word of knowledge, and, still in the dream, I had reached into the mailbox and retrieved my wedding band, my pinky ring, and my watch. Now I not only had them, but I had them on!

I began to laugh, and when Janet realized what had happened, she began to cry. When God touches me, I laugh, and when God touches Janet, she cries. Different strokes for different folks! It doesn't really matter how the glory comes; I'm just thankful when it does. Whether you laugh, cry, end up on the floor in the Spirit, or find yourself covered with golden glory, it's all wonderful. What an awesome miracle God did for us that day—a true demonstration of creative glory and of divine love!

From that day forward, the Spirit began to speak to me more and more about supernatural dreams, and I began to tell the story of this miracle whenever God led me to do so. Sometime later, I was ministering with Patricia King in Phoenix, Arizona, and I shared this testimony. After I left that conference, I recorded my first *SpiritSpa* worship album at a studio on my way back home. When I arrived home, I unpacked my bags. Janet did my laundry, and then she packed my bags again because I was scheduled to leave the following morning to minister in Cedar Rapids, Iowa.

When I got dressed the next day, I put on my wedding band and watch, but the pinky ring was missing. The reality of the situation began to sink in. I had left my pinky ring at the hotel where I had stayed while ministering in Phoenix. I was very upset about this, but there was not much that I could do about it right then. I said to Janet, "I'll have to leave for the airport. If you can, call the hotel and tell them I lost the ring and get them to send it to us." I was very concerned because the ring had been entrusted to me by my father-in-law. It had diamonds in it, and it was beautiful. It actually belonged to Lincoln. I was only wearing it until he was old enough for it to fit his finger, and then the plan was for him to pass it on to his firstborn son as well.

When I arrived in Cedar Rapids, I called Janet and asked about the ring. She said she had contacted the hotel, but they said they hadn't found anything left in the room when they'd cleaned it. "Well," I said, "you need to call them back and ask them to have a meeting with their housekeeping staff—not just one staff member, but all of them—to get them all together and confront them about this ring. I know exactly where I left it: right on the bedstand beside the bed."

Janet called the hotel back, and they were gracious enough to gather all their housekeepers together and talk to them, but each one denied ever having seen the ring. They hadn't seen the ring, and they hadn't touched the ring. None of them had the ring.

Who knows exactly what happened? I didn't know if one of them had taken the ring because they wanted it, or maybe they hadn't cleaned the room very well, and the next guest had come in and gotten the ring. I had no way of knowing. What I did know was that I didn't have the ring. And, since the hotel said they didn't have it, either, I was quite upset about it. There was nothing more that I could do.

I flew home from Iowa and picked up Janet, and we drove to the airport to catch a flight to the Fiji islands. From there, we went to New Zealand to minister. One night, while we were conducting meetings in Auckland, the Spirit prompted me to give a testimony about the miraculous return of the rings and watch. I thought to myself, "I can't give a testimony that includes the pinky ring. How can I give a testimony when I don't even know what happened to it? *I don't have the ring."*

The enemy will always attempt to steal our testimonies, but the Spirit kept urging me to share about the miracle that had occurred. I thought, "What if someone asks me where the pinky ring is now or why I don't have it on? What will I say to them?" Still, the Spirit prompted me to do it, so I finally yielded to Him and gave my testimony about the rings and watch.

After the meeting, sure enough, people came to me and asked, "Where are the rings? I want to see that pinky ring." I was embarrassed that I had been a bad steward of the miracle and had lost the ring again. So, what did I say to those who asked? "Oh, I don't have it with me right now." That was technically true. In reality, I didn't have it with me at that moment. The bad thing was that I had begun to think I would *never* have it again.

After telling people at the meeting that I didn't have the ring with me, I got all upset about the situation again. I was feeling very discouraged that I had lost a family heirloom, part of Lincoln's inheritance. When we returned to our hotel room, I began talking with Janet about it. I was wondering where I might go to buy something comparable or even half as nice as the ring I had lost. We retired for the night, but I was still sitting up in bed thinking about this when Janet fell asleep. Where could I find a good deal on a similar ring? I really didn't want another ring; I wanted *that* ring. I was so disturbed by the whole episode that, even after I fell asleep, I tossed and turned all night long. In the morning, when I woke up, I just sat in bed for a while, still feeling upset and disappointed, all because of that lost ring.

Fortunately, it was Janet's turn to minister that morning. I told her, "I'm not going down this morning. I'll just sit here in my pajamas." She went down to minister, and I continued sitting in bed thinking about the loss of my precious ring.

Then God sovereignly moved in the situation, renewing my mind. His glory started to envelop me, my thoughts began to be transformed, and I was given the assurance that He would keep me in perfect peace. Suddenly, while I was in the glory realm, I had an unusual thought. Here's the only way I can describe it: I had a picture in my mind, and I just closed my eyes and gave myself to that image. I saw a house, and I saw its front door. I went through that door and then turned left. I went through a living room, turned right, and walked through a kitchen/dining room area. Then I turned right again and went down a hallway. I could see a bathroom on the left, and there was a bedroom. I looked into the bedroom.

This was all in my mind. I wasn't caught up in a vision, I wasn't asleep in a dream, and I wasn't taken into a trance. Once more, all I can say is that it was like an idea, a thought, a picture in my imagination. I was fully aware of still being in New Zealand, sitting on the bed in our hotel room. I could hear the birds singing outside the window, and I could hear the cars driving by on the street nearby. I was completely conscious of all these things, and yet I was also aware of the image the Spirit was showing me.

In my mind, I looked into that bedroom, and I saw my ring sitting on the dresser! With my physical hand, I reached out to grab the ring. Again in my mind, I saw my hand reaching out to take hold of the ring.

Through the Spirit, I had entered into my imagination, which was now *His* imagination. He was the one engaging my thoughts. He was downloading pictures from creative glory into my mind. I was seeing what He was seeing, and I began to do what He was showing me to do.

As I reached out, I eagerly took hold of the ring, and as I did, I felt the ring coming into my physical hand. When I opened my hand, there was the ring! I was sitting in New Zealand, at the bottom of the earth, on the other side of the world from my home. My ring had come to me from North America, halfway around the globe. How did that happen? The ring was able to travel in the glory realm through multiple time zones and into another hemisphere because there is no distance and no space in creative glory. (See, for example, Acts 8:39–40.) Things can be accelerated in an instant. In God's glory, there are no limitations.

Thrilled beyond words about what had just happened, I immediately closed my eyes to see what else I might be able to grab in the Spirit. My thinking was that when the devil steals from us, he always has to repay it, with interest. But now I was being greedy, wanting something more when God had just done such an amazing miracle for me. This time, when I closed my eyes, I couldn't see a thing. There was no image. There were no revelatory thoughts.

The revelation about the pinky ring had not been my own idea. That picture had not been my own picture. It had been God's picture, and He had given me what I needed to see at the time when I needed to see it. We must always be sure to follow God's specific leading.

> THERE IS NO DISTANCE AND NO SPACE IN CREATIVE GLORY.
> THINGS CAN BE ACCELERATED IN AN INSTANT.
> IN GOD'S GLORY, THERE ARE NO LIMITATIONS.

This is just a sample of what can happen when you allow creative glory to flow into your thoughts. The Bible says, *"Let this mind be in you, which was also in Christ Jesus"* (Philippians 2:5 KJVER). God wants to download His ideas, His creativity, the possibilities of His glory realm into your imagination.

A woman in New Zealand named Jane Nieke heard my testimony about the rings and watch, and she became very excited. Many years earlier, Jane had been living in the United Kingdom, and, while she was there, she had lost a very special family brooch. It was a beautiful heirloom worth tens of thousands of English pounds, but it was priceless to her. She had lost quite a treasure!

By faith, Jane supernaturally entered into the glory realm that had been opened up through my miracle testimony. The morning after she heard me speak, she opened a drawer that she opened every morning in order to get a hairbrush to brush her hair. Lo and behold, sitting right there, in the drawer where she looked every day of her life, was that beautiful and valuable family heirloom. She had been given back a priceless treasure. How good God is!

I believe God wants to use His mind in your mind, His thoughts in your thoughts, to restore inheritances that have been stolen from *you*. As His thoughts touch your thoughts, and as His imagination touches your imagination, He will bring an abundance, a miracle, or another blessing to you.

The secret things belong to the LORD our God, but the things which are revealed and disclosed belong to us and to our children forever, so that we may do all of the words of this law. (Deuteronomy 29:29 AMP)

There is so much revelation in creative glory, so much that God is showing us, so much that He is saying, so much that He is doing—and it belongs to you as you learn to be open to it and step into it.

May the Lord give you greater spiritual dreams and heavenly thoughts than you have ever had before. May you sense the expressions of His glory and be entertained by the heavens, hearing the song of the angels and the sound of the living creatures. Even today, may you receive creative glory! Let's pray together:

Father, in the name of Jesus, thank You for fulfilling Your purposes in our lives. Thank You for bringing us visions and dreams so that we might prophesy, so that holy signs and wonders and miracles might be displayed for Your glory and honor throughout the world.

Today, we open ourselves to You and say, "Entertain us, Father! Engage our minds with Your thoughts and ways. Give us Spirit-ideas and Spirit-words." You often hear us saying that we want to move past religion and into relationship with You. We want to know Your heart and feel Your heartbeat. Thank You that, even now, You are downloading to us fresh visions from Your glory. Where we have no vision, we cannot prosper. But with Your visions and dreams, we can prosper in Your purposes. Oh, download to us Your imagination. Download to us Your thoughts and Your ideas. Download to us Your ways, for Your ways are higher than our ways. In Jesus's mighty name, amen!

CREATIVE GLORY! LET THIS GLORY ARISE IN ME!

PART II:

THE FLOW OF CREATIVE GLORY

AWAKEN THE SPIRIT SOUND

*"For as the rain and snow come down from heaven, and do not return
there without watering the earth, making it bear and sprout, and
providing seed to the sower and bread to the eater, so will My word be
which goes out of My mouth; it will not return to Me void
(useless, without result), without accomplishing what I desire, and
without succeeding in the matter for which I sent it."*
—Isaiah 55:10–11 (AMP)

From the Genesis account of creation, we know that God spoke, and the
universe was formed. (See, for example, Genesis 1:3; see also Hebrews 11:3.)
However, many believers don't realize that God is still creating through the
spoken word. Whenever and wherever God speaks, miraculous creation can
come forth.

You might be wondering, "But how, exactly, does God speak in this way
today?" Maybe you've never heard His audible voice, and you feel discouraged,
thinking that God chooses to be silent in your life. I want to share a secret
with you: you are a carrier of the divine Presence! Because you have received

forgiveness and restoration in Jesus, God now lives within you through His Holy Spirit. And one of the greatest ways in which God wants to speak new creations into being is through your lips. He wants your mouth to be filled with creative glory—His ideas, plans, and innovations—unleashing divine possibilities!

Creative glory brings self-discovery and awakening when you proactively choose to take steps to receive all that God has for you. And I have found that this self-discovery and awakening is often connected to Spirit-given prophecy, languages, and sounds.

One of the members of our church works as a teacher in the local public school system. Recently, he was sent to a teacher-training workshop where they taught him that the best way to teach children to read is by speaking a word to them first and then showing it to them. In this way, they will be able to recognize it when they see it. Hearing about this approach was a revelation to him because moving in the Spirit realm works in a similar way! God whispers a promise to our heart, and then He allows us to speak it so we can recognize it once it appears in our lives. If we want to *see* on earth what God is doing in heaven, we must first *say* what He is doing as He reveals it to us. There is a creative connection between sound and sight.

CREATIVE GLORY BRINGS SELF-DISCOVERY AND AWAKENING.

THE POWER OF LANGUAGE

Years ago, Janet and I were praying for the nation of Japan, asking God to save and bless the Japanese people. We would place our hands on a world map where the picture of that nation appeared and have faith that God would open the hearts of the people to the gospel. In addition, we decided to learn how to speak Japanese—at least some basic words, such as *konnichiwa* (hello), *arigato* (thank you), and *sayonara* (goodbye). I also learned some practical phrases, such as how to inquire for the bathroom and how to ask politely about the food. Subsequently, when we went to Japan, I was prepared to communicate, although a bit awkwardly.

We took the same approach of learning the local language when we ventured to the Canadian Arctic to serve the Inuit people there. As we were sitting around the table with some of our hosts, we asked them, "Teach us how to say hello." Their answer was *"Atelihai."* Then we said, "Teach us how to say goodbye." They answered, *"Tavvauvutit."* Next, we asked, "Teach us how to say thank you." The answer was, *"Nakurmiik."*

When you are preparing to go to another country, you should know how to speak at least some of that country's vocabulary in order to find favor with the people who live there. Whether that country is Japan, Israel, France, Costa Rica, or another nation, some knowledge of the language is important for communication and mutual understanding. Therefore, whenever we travel, we always try to learn some of the indigenous vocabulary in order to access and touch people's hearts while demonstrating respect for their native tongue.

SPIRIT-ENABLED LANGUAGES

Likewise, there are languages that give us access to the heart of God, and they are given only in the realm of creative glory. As the Spirit invites us into new places in Him and leads us there, He gives us new languages with new vocabulary for each place.

When the early Christians gathered together on the day of Pentecost, *"a rushing, mighty wind...filled the whole house where they were sitting"* (Acts 2:2 NKJV). Let me ask you: do you welcome the "suddenlies" of God when they enter your life? Do you welcome the movement of creative glory? I encourage you to invite the Holy Spirit to move in your life, saying, "Spirit, I welcome Your presence and Your glory." On the day of Pentecost, because the early believers were ready to welcome the Holy Spirit's movement, the Spirit showed up.

> *Then there appeared to them divided tongues, as of fire, and one sat upon each of them. And they were all filled with the Holy Spirit and began to speak with other tongues, as the Spirit gave them utterance.*
>
> (Acts 2:3–4 NKJV)

What happened on that day was not a natural occurrence. Creative glory gave the believers a supernatural utterance of language. Why? There were places where He wanted these believers to minister, so He was supplying a new realm of miracles for them to flow in. The Spirit of God was preparing them for a great harvest of souls. And to function in the place that the Spirit had prepared for them, these believers needed the corresponding vocabulary.

Every new realm God opens for His people requires a new language, and He is ready to supply it. Today, some believers who received the baptism in the Holy Spirit when they were very young have never gone beyond the initial spiritual language they were given at that time. However, it is important to recognize that, along our spiritual journey, God will add to the language He initially gave us, bestowing on us new words and providing us with new sounds. The God who created language has fresh and different languages to give us that will enable us to bring heaven to earth. He is an ever-increasing God who is constantly moving forward to fulfill the plans He has for us and the promises He has given us.

The Lord has a new language, a new spiritual vocabulary, for you today. All you have to do is posture yourself before the Lord and say, "God, I'm ready for a new download. I'm ready for a new language with words I have never spoken before, a supernatural language that prepares me for Your supernatural realms. I open my spirit, and I yield to You. Let Your creative glory flow through me."

One thing we must understand is that, scripturally speaking, heavenly languages are generally our entrance into all the other divine manifestations. Like the experience of the disciples in Acts 2, speaking in tongues is often the initial sign of the baptism in the Holy Spirit. (See also Acts 10.) Creative glory opens the door to heavenly realities when we are willing to yield to the Spirit and supernaturally receive the languages He desires to give us.

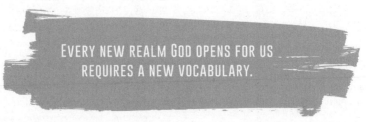

EVERY NEW REALM GOD OPENS FOR US REQUIRES A NEW VOCABULARY.

In the Spirit, there are many different tongues, or languages, available to God's people. In 1 Corinthians 12:10, they are called *"various kinds of tongues"* (ESV; see also AMP). The *New Living Translation* of the same verse says that the

Spirit of God gives people *"the ability to speak in unknown languages."* Not just one language, but multiple ones.

In the Spirit, God may give you languages that are currently spoken around the world. Or He may give you languages that are now considered ancient or extinct; they were spoken in the past but are no longer in use. People may even have forgotten these languages, but they are still known to the Holy Spirit.

The wisdom of God is reserved for the people of God. (See, for example, 1 Corinthians 2.) We are about to enter into new days in the display of God's wisdom; new days of supernatural knowing and understanding by those who love Him. This wisdom and understanding will come to us through creative glory.

SPEAKING "FOREIGN LANGUAGES"

As I described above, God may choose to enable us to speak "foreign languages." These are the languages of the nations of the world today. Of course, such tongues are not foreign to the people who speak them on a regular basis. In my experience, it is fairly common for Spirit-filled believers to receive a foreign language through the Spirit. It has happened in various places where I have ministered.

For instance, a couple of years ago, when I traveled to Albuquerque, New Mexico, for ministry meetings, my flight was late in arriving. By the time I got to my hotel, I had just enough time to change and prepare for the service. I went up to my room, and the pastors who had picked me up from the airport waited for me in the lobby to take me to the church.

As I stepped into my hotel room, a new tongue suddenly burst from my lips. I didn't actually recognize the language, but I somehow thought it might be Russian. I had never studied Russian or learned to speak it; I had only heard it spoken. However, to me, that was what my new language sounded like. The Spirit inspired me to use my smartphone to navigate to a translation app and to continue praying in the Spirit. Sure enough, the translation software recognized what I was speaking as Russian.

I sent the whole recording to my friend Marina Hertzberger. Although she is married to a German pastor and now lives in Germany, she is from

Russia and speaks her native tongue fluently. She agreed that I had spoken in Russian, and she sent me the translation. In part, the message said, "I am the Lord, and I am exalted over the nation."

> WE ARE ENTERING NEW DAYS WHEN GOD'S PEOPLE WILL DISPLAY HIS WISDOM, DAYS OF SUPERNATURAL KNOWING AND UNDERSTANDING!

This was not the first time I'd had such an experience. Sometimes, when I am singing or speaking in the Spirit, I am not aware that I am communicating in a known language, but someone who hears me will recognize what I am saying. Quite a few years ago, at a revival meeting in Canada, Janet and I and the rest of our worship team were singing in the Spirit during the worship time. Some of our singing was recorded, and we later put it on an album entitled *The Drink*, which was distributed worldwide.

That time of worship occurred just days before I was to make my first overseas ministry trip to Chennai, India. I had never studied any of the Indian languages and knew very little about India itself. However, years later, an Indian woman who heard that album recognized that what I was saying in the Spirit was the Tamil language. She was unable to get in touch with me personally, but she told my friend and fellow minister Patricia King what she had heard.

"You need to write down that translation," Patricia told her, "and I will send it to Joshua for you." So, the lady wrote down her testimony, and Patricia sent it to me. I was amazed. That woman had no way of knowing that this Spirit-given song was recorded just before I was to go to India for the first time. Creative glory truly prepares the way for you in the places where the Spirit wants to take you.

There are times when we know what God is doing in our lives, and there are other times when we don't understand the ways in which He is working. The Bible says, *"For we know in part and we prophesy in part"* (1 Corinthians 13:9, various translations). God lets us know the parts we need to know. As we are faithful to the Spirit and learn to yield to creative glory, He can do in us what we cannot do in our own abilities. In this case, God allowed me to speak in an Indian dialect that this woman needed to hear.

Something similar happened at the very end of one of the revival meetings where I was ministering in San Diego, California, when I was only about nineteen. The pastor with whom I was ministering asked me to go to the keyboard and play a bit of altar music. Often, when I was asked to do that, I was led to sing softly and gently in the Spirit. On this particular night, a woman from South America was there, and she heard me fluently speaking her Spanish dialect. She said I was giving the salvation message to her in words that were specific to her village.

That woman was sure that I didn't know Spanish, particularly the words that were unique to her hometown. Yet God knows every language and what needs to be said, when it needs to be said, and the way it needs to be said. When we yield to creative glory and speak what God is saying by the Spirit, we can stay on track with God's plan, thus allowing Him to do great things through us.

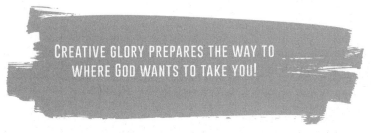

CREATIVE GLORY PREPARES THE WAY TO WHERE GOD WANTS TO TAKE YOU!

SPEAKING BY THE SPIRIT

Not long ago, I was invited by Billye Brim to be a guest on her television program, *The Prophetic Witness*. While I was sitting with Billye on the set, she shared with me about some very special things that were happening in her ministry. Among other things, she told me, "We do what we call 'Prayer Calls.' I go into the Spirit and start praying in tongues. An Arab man who had only recently been saved was listening, and he heard me praying in Arabic. He wrote down what I said and then translated it into English for me." She concluded, "I'm not sure whether other Arabic speakers would hear Arabic when I'm praying, but when this man heard it, he received a complete understanding."

Wow! That was exactly what happened with the disciples in Acts 2:

Now there were staying in Jerusalem God-fearing Jews from every nation under heaven. When they heard this sound, a crowd came together in bewilderment, because each one heard their own language being spoken. Utterly amazed, they asked: "Aren't all these who are speaking Galileans? Then how is it that each of us hears them in our native language? Parthians, Medes and Elamites; residents of Mesopotamia, Judea and Cappadocia, Pontus and Asia, Phrygia and Pamphylia, Egypt and the parts of Libya near Cyrene; visitors from Rome (both Jews and converts to Judaism); Cretans and Arabs—we hear them declaring the wonders of God in our own tongues! (Acts 2:5–11 NIV)

The people who had gathered in Jerusalem that day were confused by what was happening. They suddenly heard the humble, Galilean disciples of Jesus speaking the languages they themselves had spoken from birth. Speaking in tongues in this way is completely supernatural. As a believer speaks in the Spirit, the listener hears a clear message in their own language, without the benefit of an earthly translator. This is a spiritually creative process. It is one of the supernatural manifestations of creative glory.

Every earthly language is limited in its scope. However, heavenly languages, the languages of the Spirit, have no such limitations. There are no boundaries in the Spirit and no restrictions to what God can do through you when you are in the Spirit. When creative glory begins to flow through you, people around you may hear what you are saying in their own language, even though you don't speak that language. No wonder all the people in the crowd on the day of Pentecost were amazed! No wonder they marveled! Those who were speaking were mostly Galileans, and yet they were heard to speak many different languages.

The crowd that day was made up of Parthians, Medes, Elamites, Mesopotamians, Judeans, Cappadocians, Phrygians, Pamphylians, Egyptians, Libyans, Romans, Cretans, Arabs, and others. Both natural Jews and converts to Judaism were present, and yet they all had the same experience. They heard Jesus's followers speaking in their own languages. And what were the disciples speaking about? They were all talking about *"the wonders of God"*!

Arabs experienced this first-century miracle, and now, two thousand years later, an Arab man heard Billye Brim speak in Arabic as she prayed in the Spirit—and he translated what he had heard to the glory of God.

Let's say this prayer together now: "Lord, increase the supernatural in my life in these days! Lord, I want to receive, move in, flow in, and accelerate in the realm of Your creative glory, for I know that in Your glory, nothing is impossible."

Creative glory opens the eyes and the ears of our understanding. Creative glory speaks about our present circumstances. Creative glory prophesies about our future. Creative glory creates! God has so many ways to get our attention. And creative glory accomplishes it.

SPEAKING BRAND-NEW LANGUAGES

I believe that, by the Spirit, not only can we speak in ancient languages and in the foreign languages of our time, but we can also speak languages of the future, languages that are yet to come. The Bible tells us the following:

> *Surely the Sovereign LORD does nothing without revealing his plan to his servants the prophets.* (Amos 3:7 NIV)

You may not call yourself a prophet, but you may have a prophetic gift that God wants to ignite by creative glory. He will use it to show you things that will make a way for you in the places He intends for you to go. Recently, when I was ministering in Birmingham, Alabama, I briefly mentioned something about the possibility of our speaking future languages in the Spirit. After the meeting, a woman came to me and said, "I am a science-fiction writer, and I've had a desire in my heart to write a whole new language for the characters in the book I'm working on. I just didn't know how to get started. As you were praying over us, the language I needed began to come to me." This woman is now developing a whole new language, and it is coming to her by creative glory. In this realm, the possibilities are endless!

SPEAKING THE LANGUAGES OF HEAVEN

God may also enable us to speak languages that are spoken in heaven. The apostle Paul wrote:

> *If I could speak all the languages of earth and of angels, but didn't love others, I would only be a noisy gong or a clanging cymbal.*
> (1 Corinthians 13:1 NLT)

We know what the *"languages of earth"* are, but what are the *"languages… of angels"*? They are languages of creative glory, languages of heaven. Through creative glory, you can bring the things of heaven to earth. As you speak heavenly languages, the very atmosphere of heaven is ushered into the earthly realms.

Declare with me, "God, I want Your words. I desire Your vocabulary. Please pour out Your languages upon me!"

TENACIOUS FAITH FOR CREATIVE LANGUAGE

I met a woman on the Sunshine Coast of Australia (a beautiful area north of Brisbane) who told me how she had been very frustrated because she hadn't received the infilling of the Holy Spirit with the evidence of speaking in tongues. Many people she knew were able to speak in tongues. And many great ministers had laid hands on her and prayed for her to experience the baptism, but it seemed as if she just could not receive this blessing. Thankfully, she didn't give up but kept pressing in to the things of God.

There was a revival going on in the Sunshine Coast, and believers were gathering in a place known as the Big Pineapple, a roadside attraction built in the shape of a giant pineapple. It was once the most popular tourist attraction in Australia, drawing a million visitors every year.

When the facility faced financial issues and closed as a roadside attraction, Ben and Jodie Hughes (now based in Arizona) were led by God to rent the building for revival services. What was called the "Pineapple Revival" drew people continually for about a year and a half. If members of the public stopped to see the Big Pineapple because they didn't know that the attraction had been shut down, they were in for a big surprise because, night after night, the revival was in full force.[10]

One afternoon, while I was in the Sunshine Coast to minister at the revival, I was walking down a beach in the coastal town of Noosa Heads with Ben and Jodie and their daughter Keely. We were very surprised to see that someone had written a huge message in the sand: "MEET ME AT THE BIG PINEAPPLE AT 7 PM." The message was so large that even people standing

---

10. The Big Pineapple tourist attraction has since reopened, but not before God did a mighty work there.

at the edge of the beach could see it. Jodie commented to me, "I wonder if an angel wrote it."

This message was attracting the curiosity of people who were on the beach, and many of these people then attended the meetings at the Big Pineapple. This included the young woman who was seeking to be filled with the Spirit. She was so hungry for God that, night after night, she pressed in to get all that she could.

On one of those nights, during the worship portion of the service, this woman was pressing in to creative glory when, suddenly, in a vision, she saw a hand reaching down out of the air. This hand began writing with golden ink on one of the walls. I am hesitant to compare this manifestation to the supernatural hand that wrote on the wall during King Belshazzar's great banquet, as described in the book of Daniel, because that incident involved a judgment from God. (See Daniel 5.) However, like King Belshazzar, this woman saw a supernatural hand writing something on the wall, but she didn't understand what was being written. As she stood there trying to read what the message said, she was stunned to realize that God was giving her the heavenly language she had so desperately desired!

God has ways to reach all people. Sometimes we think He will do something a certain way, but then He does it in an entirely different way. We must allow creative glory to bring us divine results so that God will be glorified at all times. We must also accept these results and appreciate the unique ways in which they come to us.

Creative glory showed up at the Big Pineapple, and that young woman began speaking in tongues with ease as she read the golden lettering that appeared in the vision, although she did not know exactly what she was saying. As she opened her mouth to speak, at some point, her spirit began to take over, and a heavenly language overflowed from her innermost being. Since then, she has continually been able to speak in tongues.[11]

The Spirit is looking for people who have tenacious faith. There is a lot of truth to the familiar saying, "If at first you don't succeed, try, try again." As believers, we would do well to stay in the Word, press in to the Spirit, and

---

11. If you would like to be baptized in the Spirit and receive a heavenly prayer language, too, please see my book *Power Portals*. I encourage you to read it and participate in the activation provided on pages 57–60.

seek all that God has for us rather than giving up at the first disappointment. Perseverance counts when walking in faith.

You've probably heard the story of how, when Thomas Edison was conducting experiments for a type of storage battery, he kept at it through thousands of attempts, even though the research was taking months. His associate, Mr. W. S. Mallory, commented:

> This had been going on more than five months, seven days a week, when I was called down to the laboratory to see him. I found him at a bench about three feet wide and twelve to fifteen feet long, on which there were hundreds of little test cells that had been made up by his corps of chemists and experimenters. He was seated at this bench testing, figuring, and planning. I then learned that he had thus made over nine thousand experiments in trying to devise this new type of storage battery, but had not produced a single thing that promised to solve the question. In view of this immense amount of thought and labor, my sympathy got the better of my judgment, and I said: "Isn't it a shame that with the tremendous amount of work you have done you haven't been able to get any results?" Edison turned on me like a flash, and with a smile replied: "Results! Why, man, I have gotten a lot of results! I know several thousand things that won't work."[12]

Creative glory leads you to find the right solution to any difficulty. It brings a better and clearer perspective to any situation. If at first you don't succeed, try something different in God!

Someone has defined *insanity* as "doing the same thing over and over again and expecting different results."[13] Creative glory allows us to experience life through a unique lens. The flow of creative glory leads us to a process of deep growth as we learn to see things in a new light. It lifts our eyes to see as God sees. As long as we are carried by creative glory, we always have hope because creative glory cannot fail. This is encouraging to know because we may often fail at what we attempt or fall short of what we aim for.

Frances Hunter, one of my mentors in healing, told me that when the Lord first called her to the healing ministry, she laid her hands on a sick person, but

12. Frank Lewis Dyer and Thomas Commerford Martin, *Edison: His Life and Inventions*, vol. 2 (New York: Harper and Bros. 1910), 616.
13. This quote is often attributed to Albert Einstein.

that person died. I'm so glad Frances didn't stop with the first sick person she prayed for. Instead of being discouraged by that experience, she believed the Word of God that, as a believer, she was called to minister healing. She continued to lay hands on the sick, and guess what? The sick recovered, just like Jesus said they would!

For many years, Frances imparted that creative gift of healing to others—to Janet and me, and to thousands, tens of thousands, hundreds of thousands, maybe even millions of others around the world. Only God knows the scope of the ministry of Frances and her husband, Charles. They went on to write more than a hundred books, many of them about divine healing. They testified about the healings they had seen and had rejoiced over in their own ministry. However, they also explained that their whole philosophy of ministry was this: if Charles and Frances can do it, you can do it too. Perseverance will give you access to new realms of creative glory. And those realms include not only heavenly languages and earthly languages but also spiritual "sign languages."

> DON'T GIVE UP. KEEP PRESSING IN!

JESUS'S "SIGN LANGUAGES"

Several years ago, I was ministering at the Jesus School in Orlando, Florida, with my friends Michael and Jessica Koulianos, founders and directors of the school. After one of the sessions, we went out for lunch together. Michael is Greek, so we went to a wonderful Mediterranean restaurant for great food and even greater fellowship.

In the course of our conversation, which centered on the glory of God, Michael spoke about when he was a little boy and his family attended church where Benny Hinn was the senior pastor. He said that during one service, the face of Jesus, in the form of a shadow, miraculously appeared on the wall, and almost everybody there could see it. This was not a one-time event. Week after week, the face of Jesus showed up on the wall in the middle of the service, amazing all who witnessed it. Michael had tears in his eyes as he described it.

The Spirit was using this supernatural sign to get the attention of the people there and point them toward the person of Jesus. The most remarkable thing about it was that whenever Benny Hinn read the Bible, the mouth of Jesus would move, and whenever Benny stopped reading the Bible, the mouth of Jesus would stop moving. If Benny said something that was his own opinion or his own idea, the mouth didn't move, but when he again read the Word of God, the mouth moved in unison with what was being read. How could we not call this encounter a miraculous sign?

We should not be surprised when unusual signs appear in an atmosphere of creative glory. These supernatural demonstrations come to confirm the preaching of the gospel, and it is God's glory that brings these signs. Whenever signs and wonders come, we should expect many people to be drawn to Christ and receive salvation. I have seen this happen time and time again as creative glory begins to move in the midst of a meeting. God also uses such signs to bring encouragement to believers and to build our faith.

Several years ago, when I was ministering in Florida, I heard about a similar appearance of an image of Jesus at the Palma Sola Presbyterian Church in Bradenton. The face of Jesus showed up on the exterior wall of the church building, and the image was fifteen feet wide. The people of the church initially thought it might be a hoax. So, they tried to clean off the image from the wall, but they couldn't remove it, even when they tried bleach and acid. No matter what they did, the beautiful picture remained on the exterior of the church.

At the time, the sign brought many seekers to the church. Some people were just curiosity seekers, but others were genuinely hungry for God. Many stood for long periods of time in the church parking lot looking at a face of Jesus that no human being had painted and no one could remove.

This sign initially appeared more than twenty years ago. It lasted for well over a decade, and then, without warning, it disappeared. The church was very careful not to sensationalize it or create a shrine around it, and I appreciate that. We must walk lightly, valuing what God is doing while recognizing that such signs point us toward the One who sends them.

Supernatural signs are nothing new. The Bible tells of signs that were given in the past and others that will come in the future to point men and women to Christ. We are not to be sign chasers, but we know the purpose of supernatural signs—they point people to the Lord and His salvation. After all, we ourselves serve as living signs to the world around us, signs of God's love and forgiveness. (See, for example, Colossians 3:2–3.)

God wants to do extraordinary things through your life, unusual things, things that cannot be fully described or explained from a human standpoint. He wants you to be a carrier of His creative glory. And some of the ways He does this are by giving spiritual languages, by revealing spiritual signs, and by bringing other supernatural manifestations. Let's pray together for God to release His creative glory in our lives in new ways!

Father, in the name of Jesus, I thank You for Your creative glory that is flowing on earth today and awakening creative languages within us. I thank You that as Your creative glory flows, new gifts are manifesting. New anointings are being released. Fresh downloads are coming from heaven. Heavenly impartations are being deposited within us, even right now.

I thank You, Lord, for the realms of creative glory that release the unusual, the extraordinary, the unexplainable in our lives so that we can bring glory to Jesus, so that Jesus is magnified and seen, so that all eyes focus on Him for the great, wonderful, and glorious things He has done.

Lord, I thank You that creative glory is being stirred within us right now for Your purposes. Let creativity flow like a river. Your glory is rising, and You are lifting us up and causing us to accelerate into new heights, new levels, and new places in the Spirit. Reposition us, move us, communicate to us, and lift us to fulfill Your purposes. We are ready to flow with You in Your creative glory! In Jesus's name, amen.

CREATIVE GLORY! LET THIS GLORY ARISE IN ME!

UNLIMITED FLOW

*"For we are God's masterpiece. He has created us anew in Christ
Jesus, so we can do the good things he planned for us long ago."*
—Ephesians 2:10 (NLT)

What would you do if you knew that you could not fail at it?" Career
experts often ask this question of people who are seeking help finding the right
vocation. I would pose an additional question: "What would you do if you
knew that you had unlimited resources to do it with?" A hindrance that many
creative people, if not most people, struggle with is not having the resources—
financial and otherwise—to do what they feel called to do. Creative glory
has the answer to this quandary. It comes with heaven's pattern of provision,
which is like a blueprint that helps us to achieve the desired results.

A blueprint for a house clearly defines the areas where there are rooms,
stairways, doors, windows—all the features available for use in that particular
residence. Similarly, heaven's blueprint for provision includes all that the Spirit
provides for us in the glory realm, where our every need is met. I firmly believe
that creative glory releases an unlimited flow of creative provision for us.

PEANUTS, POTATOES, AND PROVISION

Years ago, I first heard the amazing story of Dr. George Washington Carver, a world-famous botanist, agricultural chemist, inventor, and educator. Dr. Carver understood the power of prayer and its importance for finding answers to the difficult dilemmas he was tasked to solve. He called his laboratory "God's Little Workshop"[14] because, in that place, he allowed creative glory to flow and bring the needed provision.

Dr. Carver was the head of the agriculture department at Tuskegee University in Alabama. To help poor farmers, he promoted ideas for preventing soil depletion, including rotating crops and diversifying beyond cotton with peanuts, soybeans, and sweet potatoes. When the farmers followed his advice, their crops produced so well that there was an overabundance of supply. Now, Dr. Carver needed another solution: what to do with the surplus of peanuts.[15]

According to biographer Glenn Clark, "Socrates consulted his demon; Seneca, his genius; Orestes, his oracle; but George Washington Carver held his intimate conversations with his 'dear Creator.'"[16] It was as a result of his personal relationship with the Holy Spirit that Dr. Carver received many downloads from creative glory. He either developed or promoted three hundred uses for the peanut and one hundred and eighteen uses for the sweet potato.[17] Applications for the peanut included "face powder, axle grease, printer's ink, milk, cream, butter, shampoos, creosote, vinegar, coffee, soaps, salads, wood stains, oil dyes, and on and on."[18]

Dr. Carver's promotion of crop rotation and alternative crops, and his development of new crop products, was life-changing for local farmers, and also reportedly for the regional and national economies. He is credited by some

14. Glenn Clark, *The Man Who Talks with the Flowers: The Life Story of Dr. George Washington Carver* (Saint Paul, MN: Macalester Park Publishing Company, Inc., 1939), 17.
15. Mary Bagley, "George Washington Carver: Biography, Inventions & Quotes," *Live Science*, December 6, 2013, https://www.livescience.com/41780-george-washington-carver.html; The Editors of Encyclopedia Britannica, "George Washington Carver," *Britannica*, https://www.britannica.com/biography/George-Washington-Carver;
16. Clark, 18.
17. George Washington Carver," *Britannica*; Rachel Kaufman, "In Search of George Washington Carver's True Legacy," *Smithsonian*, February 21, 2019, https://www.smithsonianmag.com/history/search-george-washington-carvers-true-legacy-180971538/; Bagley, "George Washington Carver: Biography, Inventions & Quotes."
18. Clark, 12.

with helping to rebuild the agricultural economy of the South.[19] Dr. Carver was invited to Washington, D.C., to testify about his work before the Ways and Means Committee of the U.S. Senate.

George Washington Carver was dedicated to serving God and humanity, saying, "It is simply service that measures success."[20] He gave his substantial life savings to Tuskegee University to create a research foundation.[21] The university writes about him, "Dr. Carver's practical and benevolent approach to science was based on a profound religious faith to which he attributed all his accomplishments."[22] Creative glory is an open heaven, overflowing with abundant provision!

NO MORE LACK

When we enter into creative glory and creative glory enters into us, there is no more lack, no more need. Why? Because God's Word says, "*And my God will liberally supply (fill until full) your every need according to His riches in glory in Christ Jesus*" (Philippians 4:19 AMP). In the ministry of Jesus, we see many examples of heavenly provision being supplied to those in need. Let's look at one of those instances:

> *When Jesus heard what had happened* [the death of John the Baptist], *he withdrew by boat privately to a solitary place. Hearing of this, the crowds followed him on foot from the towns. When Jesus landed and saw a large crowd, he had compassion on them and healed their sick.*
> (Matthew 14:13–14 NIV)

These verses demonstrate that, when Jesus sees a need, His compassion flows with miraculous provision. For many years, I've loved a saying that was sent to Janet and me in a greeting card from one of our ministry partners: "Where there is great love, there are always great miracles." Yes, where great

19. "George Washington Carver," *Britannica*; Gary R. Kremer and Carlynn Trout, "George Washington Carver," Historic Missourians, https://historicmissourians.shsmo.org/george-washington-carver; Bagley, "George Washington Carver: Biography, Inventions & Quotes."
20. Bagley, "George Washington Carver: Biography, Inventions & Quotes."
21. "George Washington Carver," *Britannica*; "George Washington Carver: A World-Famous Scientist, Inventor, and Educator," National Peanut Board, https://www.nationalpeanutboard.org/news/george-washington-carver.htm.
22. "The Legacy of Dr. George Washington Carver," Tuskegee University, https://www.tuskegee.edu/support-tu/george-washington-carver.

love flows, great miracles occur. This is why it's so important that whatever we do and whatever we create, we offer it in the Spirit of love. We know that God is love, and when the manifestation of His love comes upon us, the provision of miracles suddenly flows with great ease.

The account from Matthew 14 continues in this way:

> *As evening approached, the disciples came to him and said, "This is a remote place, and it's already getting late. Send the crowds away, so they can go to the villages and buy themselves some food." Jesus replied, "They do not need to go away. You give them something to eat."*
>
> (Matthew 14:15–16 NIV)

Isn't Jesus's response amazing? Jesus Christ came to earth as a man, but, at the same time, He was fully God. When He was among other people, His glory was present in flesh and blood. And where there is glory, there is no lack. This is why Jesus could tell His disciples there was no need to send the multitudes away. *"They do not need to go away,"* He said. *"You give them something to eat."* Creative glory was present, and so limitless provision was available.

I encourage you to stay in the flow of creative glory to receive all the provision you need. Far too many people compartmentalize their lives, separating the glory from their work life, their family life, and other aspects of their lives. They want to be in the glory, so they worship God. Then they go to work and concentrate on securing natural financial provision. There is nothing wrong with work. God gives us vocations, jobs, and assignments so that we can earn a living. Yet we must look at our occupations not as a paycheck but as a calling. When you are convinced that God has called you to your work, you will also be convinced that there is heavenly provision for that call.

> WHERE GLORY IS PRESENT, LIMITLESS PROVISION IS AVAILABLE.

PEOPLE WITH A DIFFERENCE

Throughout my life, I've struggled to fit in with other people or groups, never really conforming to the societal mold. In my opinion, many naturally creative people feel this way. We were designed to be distinct because people with a difference make a difference! Even though I've always felt like a bit of an outsider, I believe I was created to feel that way on purpose. If I felt like I completely belonged in various settings, I would never have the desire to push through boundaries and expand beyond what I already know or have experienced.

However, as I have highlighted in this book, *all* of us—not just "creative types"—have been endowed by God with creativity because we are all made in His image. The Lord can use anyone who is willing to be led beyond the mundane experiences of life or the status quo. Jesus is our ultimate example. In the Scriptures, we see Him stretching the minds of scholars and offending the rigid religious hierarchy. He walked through walls in the natural (see John 20:19), but He also did so in the Spirit—modeling how people should come together by walking straight through the racial and socioeconomic barriers of His day. His heart desired to bring all people together in the truth of God.

Jesus came to give us abundant life, and we fully discover that abundant life when we choose to live for Christ, surrendering to His creative call and receiving divine confidence from His Spirit. Frankly, I've never felt completely qualified for many tasks I've undertaken. Nonetheless, I've always felt determined to fulfill them. One of my first ministries was singing at nursing facilities with my cousin Lori when we were only six or seven years old. Grandpa and Grandma Mills had a weekly schedule of ministering at retirement communities and nursing homes, and whenever we visited our grandparents, we went with them to their ministry activities. Grandpa preached, and Grandma led the hymns. Whenever we came along, my grandparents always encouraged us to sing a Sunday school song, as special music, to bless those who were in attendance. This on-the-spot training stretched me at a young age to move out of my comfort zone to help others. It encouraged me to step up to the occasion whenever needed.

When I was a little older, I became intrigued with puppets. After watching episodes of Jim Henson's *The Muppet Show* and the outlandish shows of puppeteers Sid and Marty Krofft, I created my own puppets and performed with them at home. I guess I became really good at it because I was eventually invited to do puppet shows at church and also at my public school. So, puppeteering became my second ministry.

At the age of twelve, I confidently decided to take my show on the road. I had heard that our local Pioneer Village attraction would be celebrating a special anniversary, and I was determined to give them a call and inquire about participating with my puppets. I picked up the phone and requested to speak with a manager. It took me less than five minutes to convince them that they needed a puppet show at their big event. I got booked, and I was paid to do something I loved. This was the provision of creative glory at work in my life, and it happened before I even knew what creative glory was!

I rallied my family members and friends to help me organize, set up, and put on the show. The big day arrived, and performing at that event was a wonderful experience! Confidence is essential when it comes to creativity, and the Spirit desires to build you up in His courage. If you're confident in the Spirit, you can carry out the dreams God has put in your heart. You really can!

PEOPLE WITH A DIFFERENCE
MAKE A DIFFERENCE!

A CREATIVE WAY OF LIFE

My mother recently sent me this saying: "Being creative is not a hobby; it's a way of life." I encourage you to embrace the truth that you *are* creative and that you were made to live in the realms of creative glory. When you acknowledge this truth, you can give yourself permission to flourish where you've been planted. God created you to do what inspires and motivates you. It's what you do best!

Janet's cousin Jennifer loved knitting yet always saw it as a hobby. She worked a "regular job" during the day but looked forward to each evening when she could work on her knitting. She would knit for her friends and family; she knitted a few pieces for us on occasion. It was something that she did in her spare time, but it was what she enjoyed most.

One day, someone encouraged her to post pictures of her crafty creations on social media, and so she did, not expecting much of a result. However, her designs became so popular online that many people began requesting and paying for her creations. The result was that Jennifer's knitting has become a small business for her. Little did she realize that what she loved the most would provide for her the best!

Many people are busy working away at mundane jobs, trying to support themselves and somehow find enough money to fund their favorite hobbies. They don't realize that creative glory has been given to them to support them financially. This is the truth! Creative glory not only provides us with creative ideas, but it also provides a plan of action for those ideas to be expressed and sustained. Creative glory comes with both vision and provision.

Once we step into the creative-glory realm, we may be motivated to pick up a pencil and draw, develop a brand-new product, draw up architectural plans for an innovative building—whatever ideas are poured out into our hearts and minds. And creative glory will support us in these endeavors. You can be supported spiritually, emotionally, physically, and even financially once you find the very thing that you were placed on this earth to do. To make this discovery, ask yourself the following questions:

+ "What motivates and excites me the most?"

+ "What am I best at?"

+ "What talents, giftings, and anointings do I carry?"

Answering these questions honestly will help you to not only discover your purpose but also recognize the channel through which creative glory can overflow in your life.

Don't allow past disappointments or failures to hold you back from achieving great things. Don't allow the negative or misguided opinions of others to determine your course. God has spoken this encouragement to us through His Word:

> "For I know the plans I have for you," says the LORD. "They are plans for good and not for disaster, to give you a future and a hope."
> (Jeremiah 29:11 NLT)

All that really matters is what God has said about you and whether or not you will believe that truth. Creative glory has good plans for you, so just let go and let God do what He wants to do!

CREATIVE GLORY COMES WITH BOTH VISION AND PROVISION.

GOD KNOWS WHAT WE NEED WHEN WE NEED IT

Janet and I have three children. We also have a little fur baby whose name is Buttercup. She is a Poochon (half Toy Poodle and half Bichon Frise mix), and she has somehow become the center of attention in our home. This is probably because she is incredibly cute, just a little white ball of fluff.

We brought Buttercup into our household after our daughter Liberty was in the hospital with a serious ailment. (Thankfully, Liberty has fully recovered.) We are busy people, and we didn't need (or even want) an animal to take care of. However, one night, when I was staying in the ICU with Liberty, I could see the pain on her face. I tried to think of any way to help her, any way to relieve that pain. Without thinking, I blurted out, "Libby, when you get out of here, Daddy's going to get you a little doggy." It worked. A weak smile spread across her face, and, for that moment, the promise relieved her pain.

In the natural, I wasn't sure we were really ready to have a pet. A dog is a lot of responsibility. But it was a gift I had promised in Liberty's moment of pain, so, as a devoted father, I couldn't go back on my word. I'm convinced that every good father watches over his word to keep it. (See Jeremiah 1:12 ESV, AMP, NLT, NIV.) If he *says* it, he must *do* it. Otherwise, he loses all credibility in the family.

I can't take credit for the extensive research that was done to find the right dog for our family. All that credit goes to Janet. Moreover, no sooner did Buttercup join our family than I went back on the road for ministry trips, so Janet has been the main caregiver for our puppy. However, she would agree that Buttercup has brought our family a great amount of joy. And I have no doubt that God knew she would.

As a father, I could have felt bad about blurting out such a promise just to see a smile on my suffering daughter's face. Yet I somehow feel that God Himself caused me to say it. He knows what we need before we know it ourselves. This is another of the ways in which creative glory operates in our lives.

RIDE THE WAVE

I recently saw a spiritual vision of a gigantic wave coming our way. The Spirit told me that we must "ride the crest of the wave." The crest of anything is its highest point, so the crest of the wave would be the very top of the surge of water. That's where the Spirit said we must ride. In other words, He wants us to be positioned in the forefront of what He is doing. To be positioned in this way, we must let creative glory guide us, carry us, and prosper us.

After the Spirit said we should be riding on the crest of the wave, He added, "You should be on the cutting edge of technology." That is His will for you and me today, and it is entirely possible through creative glory.

I have a very dear friend who is a talented visual artist. I commissioned him to paint pictures of several different angels I have encountered, and He did a beautiful job. During our discussions about the artwork, he told me about a "God idea" he had recently received from the glory realm. I won't tell you all the details about it, but I was impressed. It is an absolutely brilliant idea that involves a new way to minister God's love, joy, peace, and encouragement—all through a phone app. I believe that, in the days ahead, God wants to supernaturally give His people creative ideas and technologies to help millions of people connect with His glory.

These new inventions will come from the Spirit. He was the Creator at the beginning of the world, and He's still the Creator now. Unfortunately, some modern inventions have been used by the enemy, who copies God's inventions and perverts them into demonic tools to deceive and tempt people. What the Spirit intends for good, people will often use for evil if they don't look to Him for guidance. In this hour, God needs His people to rise up like never before and bring forth *His* inventions for *His* intents and purposes. We are living in very uncertain times, and the Spirit wants us at the forefront of bringing forth the answers society so desperately needs, and to call people to turn from evil and embrace righteousness. Believers must ride the crest of the wave, standing tall at the top so that everyone can see God's glory clearly displayed through our lives.

OPEN AND READY TO RECEIVE

If our spiritual eyes and ears are open and ready to receive, we can see divine opportunities in everything. As we do what we are called to do, and as we do it under the glory cloud, we will receive divine supply. This will free us from the limitations of a paycheck and a human employer, moving us into a realm where God can bless us at all times and in all things. Hallelujah!

In the account from Matthew 14 that we looked at earlier in this chapter, the disciples saw the situation of the late hour and the hungry crowd as something they could do nothing about. Their solution was to send the people away to fend for themselves. But Jesus saw the situation as an opportunity to reveal the Father's glory. Using this circumstance to teach His disciples, He told them, *"You give them something to eat"* (Matthew 14:16 NIV). Jesus knew that the necessary provision was already there in the glory realm, even though the disciples couldn't yet see it.

> *"We have here only five loaves of bread and two fish,"* they answered. *"Bring them here to me,"* he said.   (Matthew 14:17–18 NIV)

What does this story mean to us today? It means that if we bring all of our lack to Jesus, He will reveal to us His greatness and His unlimited provision through the Spirit for those who love and serve Him.

Janet and I recently sold our home by faith, trusting in God to provide us with a new home in the location where we were moving. Not only did we sell our house, but we ended up *selling* and *sowing* the majority of our home furnishings. Initially, we sold a few items of furniture to close friends and family members. Our plan was to pack up the rest of the furnishings and bring them with us. But then the Spirit spoke clearly to us with these specific instructions: "I want you to sow them. Hold a yard sale in your driveway and allow the people who come to give a donation of any amount. Once all the items are sold and the money has been collected, take 100 percent of the money and give it away to charity. In this way, both you and others will be immensely blessed."

This was a challenge to the way we had planned to do things...but that's what happens when creative glory shows up. God brings new ideas and creative ways for you and others to be blessed. Instead of *moving* our furniture, we were to *sow* our furniture. We would not need to worry about furnishing our new house because, when we got to the place where God was calling us to go, new provision would be waiting for us. You can't out-give God!

We did exactly what the Spirit had instructed us to do. We invited friends and family to help us at our yard sale, and, within a two-hour time frame, we were able to raise thousands of dollars to sow into our local Ronald McDonald House—a charity that has been a personal blessing to our family and many other families around the world. Not only did our obedience to God's creative idea plant a seed into our future, but it also became a seed that unlocked the Spirit's revelation in others. Some friends who came to help at our sale became inspired to clear out their home and make way for the blessings of God to flow into their own lives. Just yesterday, they sent us this message: "We got rid of a lot of stuff and gave a lot of stuff away! And we literally threw our poverty mentality in the garbage at the dump!"

> IF WE BRING ALL OF OUR LACK TO JESUS,
> HE WILL REVEAL TO US HIS GREATNESS AND HIS UNLIMITED
> PROVISION THROUGH THE SPIRIT FOR THOSE WHO LOVE AND SERVE HIM.

Boldly yield to God your entire life—with all of its limitations—and He will enrich and expand it with His goodness. If you are living an impoverished lifestyle, submit that lifestyle to the creative glory of God. Without embarrassment, say to Him, "God, here I am. I have yielded myself to You. Come and speak to me about what I must do to change my situation. Minister to me and show me what I need to release to You. Bring revelation about how I can take what I have and see it multiplied for Your use."

"*Bring them here to me*" (Matthew 14:18 NIV), Jesus said. When we do what we can do—and bringing what we have to Jesus is what we can do—God will do what only He can do.

THE GLORY REVEALED

After the disciples brought to Jesus all the food they had, Jesus took charge and began to reveal the Father's glory:

> *And he directed the people to sit down on the grass. Taking the five loaves and the two fish and looking up to heaven, he gave thanks and broke the loaves. Then he gave them to the disciples, and the disciples gave them to the people. They all ate and were satisfied, and the disciples picked up twelve basketfuls of broken pieces that were left over. The number of those who ate was about five thousand men, besides women and children.*
> (Matthew 14:19–21 NIV)

As the disciples moved in faith by distributing the food Jesus had given back to them, the supernatural multiplication took place. We must learn how to take charge of situations through creative glory, again using Jesus as our

example. Jesus sat the people down and prayed. After this, the abundant provision began, and everyone was fed. This is creative glory! It is the life-giving
energy of God, and it's not just for when we are in church. It is for every moment
of every day, wherever we happen to be. Learn to rest in God's presence, for it is
His presence that brings divine provision wherever it is needed.

Jesus *"gave thanks"*—and that is a key to resting in the glory. God gives us
the opportunity to reflect on His faithfulness in our lives. It is a good practice
to write down the many, many things He has blessed you with. This is a powerfully positive act compared with merely complaining and saying, "Oh, I'm
so poor. I don't have a thousand fish. I don't even have a hundred fish to my
name." Instead of focusing on lack, focus on the blessings you *do* have. "I am so
blessed because I have five loaves and two fish!" That's a very different attitude.
Give thanks for the little you have, and it will be multiplied in creative glory.
An attitude of gratitude brings plentitude.

We should all spend time each day resting in the glory, reflecting on our
blessings, and thanking God for His provision. Thanksgiving opens a supernatural portal in the Spirit. That's why the psalmist wrote the following:

> Enter his gates with thanksgiving and his courts with praise; give thanks
> to him and praise his name. For the LORD is good and his love endures
> forever; his faithfulness continues through all generations.
>
> (Psalm 100:4–5 NIV)

Supernatural gates open to us when we are thankful. I declare that plenty
is coming to your life and that the Spirit is bringing it to you through creative
glory. Again, it doesn't make any sense to sit and complain about what you
don't have. That's easy to do, but it gets you nowhere. Complaining doesn't
bring blessing. If you insist on focusing on lack and grumbling about it, you
will never develop the spiritual sight you need to do God's will. God wants to
give you eyes to see the abundance that surrounds your life. Such vision only
comes within a creative flow, and great faith brings just such a flow. Jesus said,
"According to your faith be it to you" (Matthew 9:29 KJVER).

My friend Bonita Bush, an anointed minister, wrote about how the Spirit
provided for her in an unusual way when she entered into the divine supply of
the creative-glory realm:

I opened the refrigerator door and faced the reality of the stark circumstances. Looking at the wide-open spaces on the shelves, it took no imagination for me to realize that *I had only one day's worth of food left*! Not only that, but there was seemingly no relief in sight, no relief from this long, desolate season of job loss, depleted savings, an empty bank account, and nowhere and no one to turn to. The natural realm was not being kind to me. My heart sank, and the knot in the depths of my stomach began to tighten.

Then I heard the words, "Speak fishes and loaves over your refrigerator." From deep within me, those words began to resonate as I stared at the near-empty refrigerator. My lips took on the words, and I slowly began to speak.... I spoke those words over my refrigerator, commanding and demanding, over and over throughout the day. I realize now, even though I didn't realize it then, that I was commanding the heavens to release the treasure of food into manifestation to supply my desperate need.

Each time I went to the refrigerator that day, a remnant of food was there, and it was always enough to fill my stomach. Yet there was always more when I returned. Even the next morning, when I opened the refrigerator, there it was, enough food for the day! I ate my fill, still not realizing the full impact of how God had answered my prayer.

Day after day, I would repeat this declaration in faith as I grasped the handle of the refrigerator door: "In the name of Jesus, I speak fishes and loaves over this food in my refrigerator. Lord, thank You for this food that fills my stomach." My heart was focused on expectation.... Each day the food would fill me and yet show no evidence of either depleting or multiplying. It was just there![23]

Recognize that the answers to your prayers are coming—and will come in a creative way. In the natural, this might seem impossible, but we must refuse to look at what is seen and instead look at what is unseen. (See 2 Corinthians 4:18.) Lift your sights higher and start thanking God for what He is doing

---

23. Bonita Bush, *His Passion to Provide: Heavenly Deposits, Multiplication, and Reserves of Heaven* (Maitland, FL: Xulon Press, 2021), 1. This excerpt has been edited for this publication.

in your life. He has done much for you already. He has brought you through many difficult places and given you many gifts. Being grateful and thanking Him will open more doors of blessing for you.

I want to follow up on what happened after Janet and I had our big yard sale and moved to our new location, trusting God to provide us with a home and furniture. The area where we relocated was a seller's market, with many homes selling for tens of thousands of dollars above the listing price. But in a remarkable way, God orchestrated a divine connection so that we moved into a beautiful new home, paying much less than the listing price. Our real estate agent even commented, "Wow! It is a miracle!"

And in the way that only He can do, God filled our home with new furniture of all kinds—a dining room table, chairs, chandeliers, bed frames, everything that we needed and more! Our home is now fully furnished; not one of the rooms lacks anything. And, to top it off, all the furniture is even better than the furniture we sowed, even though that furniture was the nicest we had owned up to that point. Again, when we follow the Spirit's leading and enter into the unlimited flow of creative glory, there is never any lack. This pertains to spiritual, emotional, and physical blessings in our lives.

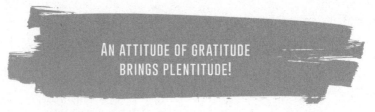

AN ATTITUDE OF GRATITUDE
BRINGS PLENTITUDE!

OUR PROVIDER TODAY AND TOMORROW

God's provision is especially apparent during difficult times. He wants His creative glory to flow from our lives in such a vibrant way that people will marvel at it. They will wonder why the troubles of the world that are adversely affecting so many people are *not* affecting the people of God. When we have faith, a situation that is a problem for the world does not need to be a problem for us. Why? Because we live on the crest of the wave, at the top, in the highest place of creative glory.

At the height of the coronavirus pandemic, unemployment suddenly soared, and it was an uncertain time worldwide. Our son, Lincoln, was eighteen, and he was working at an ice cream parlor. For some reason, ice cream was deemed an "essential service," so Lincoln continued to have a job. All the kids who came into the ice cream shop loved him. They called him the "Ice Cream Man" and always asked for the "Linc Special"—Lincoln's special concoction of particular ice cream flavors and mix-ins.

One day, when Lincoln was at home, he was going to his bedroom, and he passed Janet and me in the kitchen. I'll never forget what happened next.

"Hey, Dad and Mom," Lincoln said.

"Yeah?"

"I really feel like the Spirit's been telling me to do something."

This caught my interest, and I asked him, "Well, what is it that the Spirit has told you to do?"

"The Spirit spoke to me and told me that I need to sow a very significant seed into your ministry."

As you can imagine, this really touched our hearts. Our son wanted to sow into the work of God in our lives. What a blessing! What blessed me most was that Lincoln said, "The Spirit spoke to me," and also that he had listened and was choosing to flow in obedience to the Spirit's voice. That is the key! If we listen to what the Holy Spirit tells us to do, and we're willing to give what the Spirit is asking us to give—whether it is our time, devotion, creativity, or finances—we are positioning ourselves in the flow of creative glory.

Lincoln did what the Spirit had spoken to him. The next day, when he came home from work at the ice cream store, he had a bounce in his step. "Dad," he said, "you'll never believe what happened today. I was just promoted to shift supervisor." He was beaming!

God is so good. When we listen to and obey His instructions, He is faithful in ways we may not see coming. The next promotion can be yours if you stop looking at things in the natural, focus your eyes on the Spirit, and say yes to Him. God will do the rest, and He will do it in a creative way that you could never have imagined. Creative glory will flow with provision for you!

CREATIVE GLORY! LET THIS GLORY ARISE IN ME!

ANGELS OF CREATIVITY

*"The heavens are telling of the glory of God; and the expanse
[of heaven] is declaring the work of His hands."*
—Psalm 19:1 (AMP)

Several years ago, while I was ministering in Jerusalem, the Spirit spoke a prophetic word through me. This word was about angels being dispatched to help God's people overcome the difficulties they were facing. The entire prophecy is found in my book *Angelic Activations*. Here is a portion of what the Spirit said:

> I am releasing and dispatching My angels over your life right now.... Many angels are being released, for I have commanded My angels concerning you, and they shall work with those who are open and ready to work with them.
>
> ...Open your spiritual senses fully and prepare to see My Spirit moving in your midst in a new way. Angels are being dispatched for My purposes. Spirit winds are beginning to blow once again, and you

may even feel the brush of their wings. Wingtip to wingtip, they are gathering all around you.[24]

Today, the world needs solutions to numerous crises and dilemmas. And when God's people dwell in creative glory, being open to the work of God's angels, they are adept at finding such solutions. In the days ahead, you can be sure that God will do utterly amazing things for each of us as we stay connected to Him and to His heavenly provision toward us through the ministry of angels. Throughout the Bible, we see God utilizing His angels in creative ways and on creative assignments. They've fulfilled many roles, from cake baker (see 1 Kings 19:5–6) to lion trainer (see Daniel 6:22) to pro wrestler (see Genesis 32:24). They're able to do whatever God requires of them.

One thing I know for certain about angels is that they love to be involved in God's creative work on earth. They come from the realm of creative glory and serve to bring glory to the Lord. The angels not only love to be involved in God's creative work, but they love to be involved in our creative activities as well. I believe angels are being dispatched to assist everyone who truly wants to work with God.

It's important to remember that, although angels are spiritual beings, they haven't always existed. They had a beginning, just like we did, being created by God to praise and worship Him as well as to carry out His assignments. This is why we should be very careful never to worship angels, pray to them, or idolize them in any way. We worship only God, our Creator, and give Him all the glory that He deserves. However, angels assist those who belong to the Lord and who look to Him for help. We can acknowledge angels when they come into our lives because they are sent by almighty God for a divine purpose.

Are they [angels] *not all ministering spirits, sent forth to minister for them who shall be heirs of salvation?* (Hebrews 1:14 KJVER)

CREATIVE GLORY IS FLOWING,
AND THE ANGELS ARE BEING RELEASED.

---

24. *Angelic Activations: A Scriptural Look at the Modern-Day Ministry of Angels* (New Kensington, PA: Whitaker House), 24–25.

PARTNERING WITH CREATIVE ANGELS

I recently received a testimony about creative angels from a young man named Freddy. He had attended one of the Angel School seminars that we held at Warner Bros. Studios in Burbank, California. I love hosting spiritual seminars, especially in locations where a lot of creative people live and work, because God desires to fill such places with His creative glory. Here is what Freddy wrote to me:

> I just wanted to share a pretty cool testimony with you. Last year at the Angel School you held at Warner Bros. Studios with your wife, I was tremendously blessed. I also recall your wife ministering to me toward the end and saying that I would partner up with a creative angel that has been assigned to me. Anyway, the past couple of months I really feel like God has given me a whole new level of creativity, and I have been partnering up with this creative angel. It's as if so much more passion and clarity has come to me…. I didn't even know you could partner up with a creative angel, but I love how God's word has come to fulfillment.

Freddy was experiencing what it is like to be assisted by a creative angel who has been specifically assigned to help you in your God-given assignments. There is an entire class of angels that focuses on the arts and other creative endeavors in all areas of life. I call these heavenly beings "angels of creativity."

+ There are angels that provide creative ideas for winning the lost. I call them soul-winning angels.

+ There are angels that prepare and serve spiritual food. I call them baking angels.

+ There are angels that write and that strengthen writers. I call them scribe angels.

+ There are angels that sing and play heavenly instruments. I call them music angels.

+ There are angels that artistically decorate and inspire artists. I call them painting angels.

+ There are angels that deliver designs, plans, and maps. I call them architect angels.

+ And there are many more!

I think many of these designations are open to interpretation, but all of these angels minister to God. And, when they are assigned to do so, they also minister to God's people. They are commissioned to work with us in various creative projects. Over the years, I have personally interacted with many such angels. Whatever you're called to do, God has angels prepared to help you do it in a supernatural way. You never need to feel alone again.

Often, creatives can feel misunderstood or lonely in the path that they're traveling. However, once they receive the revelation about the presence of creative angels, they can be comforted to know that God has placed these angelic beings alongside them on that path. There's a nice saying that goes, "An angel in the house, they say, will guard your family night and day." However, you should see God's angels not just as your spiritual guardians, but also as your artistic assistants. They are there to bring you divine encouragement and help—to "lift your arms" when you feel weary. (See Exodus 17:10–13.)

One of the few angels specifically named in Scripture is Gabriel, and among the Hebrew meanings of his name is "God is my strength."[25] I want you to realize that if you've felt worn out or drained in your creative call, God has angels available right now to minister His strength in your area of need. They can also help inspire the gifts of God that have lain dormant inside you due to creative blockages. Receive this angelic ministry!

Divine inspiration is available to you whenever you need it. Angels are being released to minister God's purposes in your life. You may feel the presence of angels as a warmth resting on the top of your head or as a gentle heat moving across your shoulders and down your spine. Or you may experience what feels like a slight electrical tingling flowing over your body. At such times, if you close your eyes for a moment, it will help you focus better on what is happening around you in the Spirit realm. Don't force it, and don't try too hard. Just relax and appreciate the moment.

Again, angels love God's glory, and the more of His glory that you absorb into your life, the more angelic activity you will experience. I declare that, right now, the glory of God is flowing through you. His creative glory is with you, moving in your life.

---

25. Don Stewart, "Who Is the Angel Gabriel?" Blue Letter Bible, https://www.blueletterbible.org/faq/don_stewart/don_stewart_25.cfm.

> ### DIVINE INSPIRATION IS AVAILABLE TO YOU WHENEVER YOU NEED IT.

DIVINE INSPIRATION

I have to believe that, throughout history, many artists often saw things in the spiritual realm. This may explain their fascination with painting angels and other heavenly beings in their masterpieces. The famous renaissance artist Michelangelo reportedly said, "I saw the angel in the marble and carved until I set him free."[26] Artists know how to open the eyes of their imaginations to see into the unseen realm, and creative glory helps open our eyes to see into the unseen realm of *God's imagination.* Creative glory brings creative vision, which is the art of seeing what is invisible to others. When we receive this ability, we can learn to do amazing things with great ease.

A vital aspect of flowing in creative glory and working with God's angels of creativity is the dimension of prayer. Today, the Spirit is revealing to us the importance of seeking the Lord before taking on any creative task. Through prayer—in which our hearts are united with God's heart in mutual love and purpose—we can receive divine solutions and find new and easier ways of accomplishing difficult tasks. Through prayer, supernatural doors are opened in our spirits to enable us to embrace deeper heavenly realities, and our spiritual eyes are opened to see into the unseen realm.

From the Scriptures, it is clear that when God's people pray, heaven shows up. And one of the common ways in which heaven arrives is by the ministry of creative angels. Whether you see these heavenly beings doesn't change the truth that, through prayer, they have been commissioned, activated, and released to bring you into the promise that God has spoken to you.

There were instances in which Abraham and Moses prayed, and, as a result, angels saved God's people and destroyed their enemies. (See Genesis 18:1–19:29; Exodus 14.) Jesus Himself activated angels through prayer. He prayed on the Mount of Olives during His time of trial before His arrest and crucifixion, and an angel from heaven appeared and strengthened Him. (See Luke 22:39–46.)

26. "Quotes of Michelangelo," Michelangelo, https://www.michelangelo.org/michelangelo-quotes.jsp.

In Acts 2, what happened when the believers were praying together? There was the sudden presence of supernatural wind and fire. A mighty, rushing wind was heard, and spiritual tongues of fire rested upon the disciples. This result should not surprise us because, as the books of Psalms and Hebrews reveal, "[God] *makes His angels winds, and his ministering servants flames of fire*" (Hebrews 1: 7 AMP; see Psalm 104:4). I believe that, as the early Christians prayed, angels showed up as wind and fire. Through these manifestations, the Holy Spirit had His own procession, His own parade, upon His arrival at Pentecost. It was a heavenly demonstration of the truth that He had come. The blowing of the wind and the falling of the fire said, "The Spirit is here! Pay attention! Open yourselves and receive!"

WHEN GOD'S PEOPLE PRAY, HEAVEN SHOWS UP—
MANY TIMES THROUGH MINISTERING ANGELS.

The angelic ministry to and with the New Testament church began on that day of Pentecost, ushering in the divine presence of the Spirit. It was in that amazing moment that the believers were filled with creative glory that enabled them to speak new languages, work miracles, and share the gospel with power.

WHAT ARE ANGELS LIKE?

When it comes to angelic ministry in the lives of believers, you may have the following questions:

+ What does an angelic encounter involve?

+ Can we clearly see angels?

+ What do angels look like?

The Bible indicates that angels may appear in various forms. Some angels have wings, but, in my own personal experience, most do not. Actually, most angels don't look like our common idea of angels at all. Instead, they may appear as men, as a flaming fire, or in a myriad of other ways. The writer of Hebrews tells us to be hospitable to other people because, at any given moment, we might entertain angels and not even know it. (See Hebrews 13:2.)

I have seen angels that were just as real as if I were seeing another human being. Sometimes I see golden angels walking beside me. These angels come with divine, supernatural provision—supplies from heaven's abundance— and they sprinkle golden glory over me. However, more often, I see angels like a superimposed image or a silhouette on top of what I see in the natural world. Sometimes I see an angel's faint outline standing in front of me, usually just enough to let me know it is near. At other times, I feel winds blowing in the Spirit, and I know there is angelic movement close by.

I might also see orbs of colored lights—usually gold, purple, or white, but other colors as well. The Lord showed me that when I see these orbs, I'm not seeing an actual angel but rather the specific gift or impartation an angel is holding or bringing. Red orbs represent the blood of Jesus and a healing flow. Gold orbs symbolize the prosperity and glory of God. White signifies purity and holiness. Purple represents royalty and the abundance of new wine. When I am preaching and I see such orbs, I know that angels are present to bring me needed impartations, and I minister to people in a corresponding way.

ANGELS IN THE CLOUDS

People often come to my meetings very excited to show me photos they have taken of the clouds. Their photos contain cloud formations in angel-like shapes. Some of the cloud-angels are wispy, with large, outstretched wings, while others are more fluffy and dense, with what appears to be a sword or some other object in their hands.

I'm always impressed when people have a passion for the Lord and His kingdom, and I think it's wonderful when they keep their eyes open to see Him and His glory in the world around them. However, until a few years ago, I didn't pay much attention to potential spiritual manifestations in clouds. I had never seen angels in clouds or personally connected to what God might be doing in the glory realm through the appearance of cloud-angels. I knew that angels and clouds were sometimes mentioned together in the Scriptures. (See, for example, Revelation 10:1; 14:15.) And I also knew that when Jesus ascended to heaven, both a cloud and angels were involved:

And after He said these things, He was caught up as they looked on, and a cloud took Him up out of their sight. While they were looking intently into the sky as He was going, two men in white clothing suddenly stood beside them. (Acts 1:9–10 AMP)

In the above passage, what appeared to be *"two men"* were actually two angels sent to bring a very special message to the early believers. They were fulfilling one of the roles of angels—delivering messages from God to His people.

As I mentioned, even though I understood the biblical connections between angels and clouds, I'd never seen a direct association between them myself. However, several years ago, I had an experience that completely rocked my perspective on this. It came in the form of a unique heavenly message from a creative angel.

One day, my daughter Liberty was feeling under the weather. She had stayed home from school and was lying ill in her bunk bed. Both Janet and I had prayed for her and were believing that her sickness would leave quickly, and yet there she lay in her bed. My home office was just down the hall from her bedroom upstairs. I went to work in my office, but I kept both my door and Liberty's bedroom door open so that I could hear her if she needed my attention.

I can't remember exactly what I was working on at the time, but I do remember that I was sitting at my desk, which faced a large floor-to-ceiling window that was open and had a beautiful view of the neighborhood. The sky was clear and blue, with a few fluffy, white clouds floating high above the houses. Looking outside, I began to think about some of the cloud-angel photos I had recently seen. Again, I was happy for others to be delighted with them, but I wasn't really sure that these pictures were of real angels. Maybe they were just cloud formations that captured people's creative imaginations.

As I was thinking about this, the clouds in front of my window suddenly began to form into a very clear image that appeared to be an angel, lying on its side, smiling at me with the biggest grin. Then he waved his hand at me as if to get my attention!

I was in shock. What in the world was happening? I blinked my eyes a few times, trying to comprehend if what I was seeing was really taking place. How could this be? But there it was: an angel appearing in a cloud formation. It was apparent to my spirit that this was very real and that it was happening for me. In that moment, without trying to muster any faith of my own, I knew exactly what to do. I understood that this was a healing angel sent by God, and it was ready to be commanded for service. So, I said, "In the name of Jesus, go and bring healing to Liberty."

When I spoke, just like that, the image vaporized, and the cloud was gone. The next thing I knew, Liberty was calling out from her room, saying, "Mommy, I'm feeling really good. Can I get out of bed?" That angel had ministered God's healing to Liberty in an accelerated way, and she received an instant miracle. Through this amazing experience, the Spirit taught me to be more open to the creative ways in which His angels can appear to us. I'm not saying that every cloud you see in the sky is an angel, but it is possible for angels to appear in unusual ways. And when they do, you will know it by the confirmation of the Spirit.

ANGELS AMONG WORSHIPPING BELIEVERS

A woman named Mary used to attend many of our meetings at Calvary Pentecostal Tabernacle in Ashland, Virginia, and she always had a camera in hand, ready to catch the supernatural activity that took place in the tabernacle during the daily camp meetings. This always blessed me about Mary: she was continually ready for God to make an appearance in His glory. Like Mary, you and I should be ready to see the heavens displayed before us!

Many times, after my sessions, Mary would show me the photos she had taken in the heavy glory atmosphere, and they were marvelous to see. There were angels, light orbs, faces of the *great cloud of witnesses* (Hebrews 12:1 NIV), and other supernatural appearances, all captured in her photography.

One time, when I was ministering at the fiftieth anniversary celebration for the camp, Mary's camera captured the seraphim as they made a dramatic appearance across the platform. They came into the meeting like swooshes of vibrant, flaming fire. This is the way they appear, for their name means "burning."[27] For some reason, it seems that digital cameras pick up on glory-realm activity much more than traditional cameras do. Mary caught it all.

---

27. *Strong's Exhaustive Concordance of the Bible*, #H8314.

STARS IN THE NIGHT

Recently, our friend Joe Garcia came over to our house, and while he was standing near the island counter in our kitchen, he looked up and saw what he described as "sparkling stars" bursting forth in the atmosphere all around him. When he began sharing what he was seeing, I knew immediately what it was, and he did too. We both agreed that he had encountered the presence of God's angels in our home. This manifestation has a biblical basis because that's one of the ways Job described the angels:

> *The morning stars sang together and all the sons of God (angels) shouted for joy.* (Job 38:7 AMP)

The Hebrew word for *"stars"* in this verse is *kokab*, one of the meanings of which is "a prince."[28] The same word is used in Judges 5:20 in reference to the warrior angels that fight against spiritual enemy forces. Thus, God has a class of angels that are described in the Bible as "stars." They operate in the cosmic second heaven and may appear bright in the midnight sky. (William Shakespeare, describing the stars of the sky, said, "Each in its motion like an angel sings."[29])

The Spirit wants us to understand the implications of angelic beings being called "stars." Even when we feel as though we're blinded by our current conditions, or feeling a stubborn blockage in creativity, God has His stars shining in the darkest night. Angels come to help transition us from the midnight of feeling without hope into the dawn of fresh spiritual awakening. If you're presently in the dark of night, look for the "stars." They're right there, pushing back against demonic warfare and shining for you.

I have sensed the presence of angels as I have been writing this chapter. Let's pray before we continue:

> Lord, I thank You that You have commissioned angels of creativity to come from heaven with creative impartations for us. We lift our hands right now and receive Your creative glory. Amen!

---

28. *Strong's*, #H3556.
29. *The Merchant of Venice*, Act 5, Scene 1.

> EVEN WHEN WE FEEL AS THOUGH WE'RE BLINDED BY OUR CURRENT CONDITIONS, OR FEELING A STUBBORN BLOCKAGE IN CREATIVITY, GOD HAS HIS STARS SHINING IN THE DARKEST NIGHT.

GUIDED BY CREATIVE ANGELS

Angels of creativity are being dispatched into our lives to help us in creative ways as we choose to live in the rhythm of creative glory. In the Bible, we see that God's people were guided by angels on various occasions, and these angels came in creative ways: through visions, dreams, or otherworldly manifestations. Here are some examples:

+ The Israelites were led by an angel through the wilderness into the promised land. (See Exodus 14:19; 23:20.)

+ Joseph received guidance from an angel that appeared in the night. (See, for example, Matthew 2:13.)

+ The early apostles were led out of prison through angelic intervention. (See Acts 5:17–19; 12:1–11.)

+ The apostle Philip obtained specific directions for his ministry from an angel. (See Acts 8:26.)

+ The centurion Cornelius received an angelic message from God that led him and his household to hear the gospel and receive salvation. (See Acts 10.)

God wants us to become more sensitive to spiritual matters and supernatural movement. First and foremost, we should be led by the Spirit of God who lives within us. However, we must also allow God's angels to bring us guidance and confirmation along the way. Proper spiritual direction is important, and, among other things, angels are able to help guide us in matters of creativity. Often, the way we are guided by angels is by paying attention to the gentle nudges they offer us as we choose to walk in the Spirit.

One day, as Janet and I were sitting at my office desk, tiny feathers began falling from above us, one after another. As they appeared and gently floated through the air, we had to take notice. There was no natural reason for why the feathers were appearing, and yet there they were, falling all around us. Such an occurrence is not uncommon for us. It happens frequently in our daily lives, but it also occurs as we minister publicly or online through our weekly *Glory Bible Study*.

What does this manifestation indicate? Feathers are reminders that angels are always near. When I see feathers appearing in a seemingly supernatural way, it signifies to me that angels are at work in our midst. By God's Word, we already know that angels are working on our behalf, but these signs come to remind us of that truth. I am believing for an increase in angelic activity wherever you are. Feel it swirling around you even now. May your home and life be filled with the creative angels of God.

Jesus taught us, *"But seek first his kingdom and his righteousness, and all these things will be given to you as well"* (Matthew 6:33 NIV). We are to seek God's kingdom *"first."* This means we must stay focused on Jesus, and then *"all these things will be given to [us]."* *"All,"* of course, means everything, exclusive of nothing. What are *"all these things"*? Anything and everything we need—and much of that need can be supplied through angelic intervention. The supply comes from God as we live for Christ, but it is often delivered by His holy angels.

CREATIVE ANGELIC SOLUTIONS

Creative glory brings a creative solution for every need, and angels are always ready to help God's people win their spiritual battles in creative ways! Acts 12:1–19 describes how Jesus's disciple Peter was thrown into prison. It seemed like a dismal situation. James had already been executed for his faith, and when Herod saw that this pleased some of the people, he commanded that Peter be detained as well. The only reason he didn't kill Peter immediately was that it was Passover, a holy, solemn time for the Jews. Herod's plan was to quickly bring Peter to trial after the festival.

The Bible tells us very clearly that the night before Herod was to execute Peter, the believers were engaged in serious prayer. This was not a time when they were reading prayers from a book. They were not reciting classic prayers they had said many times before. Those who were interceding were the same believers who had encountered the power of the Holy Spirit on the day of Pentecost. These men and women knew that when trouble came, they needed to pray—and not just any prayer. They prayed in the Spirit with creative glory bubbling up from their innermost being.

As the believers prayed, an angel appeared as a bright light inside Peter's prison cell. The result was a creatively supernatural jailbreak! Peter was delivered from bondage, which allowed him to continue to preach the gospel for many years to come.

I urge you to read the entire twelfth chapter of Acts. What is recorded there is absolutely remarkable. It depicts creative glory at work in amazing ways. What happened to Peter can happen to you too. If you need a breakthrough, then pray in the Spirit, expecting God's creative glory to appear on the scene. The Lord may choose to send an angel, or angels, to assist you.

Praying in the Spirit is one of my favorite activities. I pray in the Spirit while preparing for the day. I pray in the Spirit when I walk down the street. I pray in the Spirit while driving my car. During these times, I often sing in tongues, encouraging myself in the Holy Spirit.

When we pray in the Spirit, we go beyond our natural limitations and intercede from the realms of glory. We pray past our circumstances by using God's creative vocabulary. God gives us heavenly languages to bring forth manifestations from heaven in our homes, businesses, communities, or wherever the need may be. You may not even be aware of it, but the Spirit praying through you might invite angelic hosts to come to your rescue in a creative way. In response to our Spirit-inspired prayers, angels might show up in the middle of any creative blockage we are experiencing to help bring fresh ideas, new concepts, and heavenly inspiration. When you open your spirit and soul to receive the creative flow of heaven, God's messengers can respond in the blink of an eye.

> THE HOLY SPIRIT,
> PRAYING THROUGH YOU,
> MAY INVITE ANGELIC HOSTS TO COME TO YOUR RESCUE!

The Spirit fills you and supernaturally equips you for service to God. Then angels come to surround you and assist you in those acts of service. This is how the Holy Spirit and angels work together to ensure that you have everything you need to do what you are called to do.

TYPES OF CREATIVE ANGELS

Earlier, I mentioned several specific types of creative angels. Let's look in more depth at several of these: soul-winning angels, scribe angels, and music angels.

SOUL-WINNING ANGELS

One of the areas that angels help us with is winning souls for Christ in creative and unusual ways. Several years ago, my friend Linda Keough had a special vision from the Lord about an activity in the Spirit realm. She was so excited about it that she wrote and told me what she had seen:

> As a friend was praying for souls being added to the Book of Life, I saw a white, feathered ink pen. Then, I saw a book and a hand with the pen in it. It was God's hand, writing the new names into the Book of Life. Then, I saw another hand on top of His hand, and it was ours, joining together with God, signing those names that were being added. It was so amazing and awesome. I already knew that we co-labored with the Kingdom, but it was such an honor to know that we have our hand connected with God's hand, signing new believers into the Book of Life when we win souls for Christ. God is so good!

The message of this vision was a great revelation to Janet and me. It was eye-opening, enabling us to understand that there is a very real connection in the Spirit realm between what happens on earth and the purposes of the eternal kingdom of God. In the life of a believer, winning souls for Jesus is of utmost importance, and God desires to give us creative glory for that task.

Many years ago, Charles and Frances Hunter, who were my spiritual mentors, were having lunch at a restaurant in a small town in Missouri when an unknown gentleman sat down at their table and shared a very special supernatural key with them. He said, "As soon as the waitress gets to the table, I will say to her, 'There are two kinds of waitresses: those who are saved and those who are about to be. Which one are you?'" Frances was fascinated by the question because it doesn't give the person an out! She instantly recognized that it is a win-win situation; there is no way you can lose. If the person is not saved, the only other answer they can give you is, "I am about to be."

Excited about the opportunity to use this new soul-winning technique, Frances told the stranger that she would ask the waitress the question herself in order to try it out. When the waitress came to the table, Frances asked her, "There are two kinds of beautiful waitresses who work in this restaurant: those who are saved and those who are about to be. Which one are you?" The waitress started crying and said, "I guess I'm the last one."

Frances was holding the woman's hand and didn't let go. Next, she said, "Wonderful! Repeat this after me," and she led the waitress in the sinner's prayer: "Father, forgive my sins. Jesus, come into my heart and make me the kind of person You want me to be. Thank You for saving me today."

The waitress repeated the prayer and then burst into tears. Frances asked her, "Where is Jesus right now?" and she replied, "In my heart!" It was a glorious experience. In that moment, the Hunters learned that it was easy to win people to Jesus! Every person you meet is an opportunity to share the gospel, and creative glory will guide you with just the right words to say.

Frances later told me she believed that the gentleman who had sat down with them at the table that day was an angel. The stranger had looked like an ordinary man, but even though they didn't know him, he felt comfortable enough to invite himself to sit down at their table. Then he disappeared without anyone immediately noticing that he had left. God has angels of creativity available at any given time to help us learn heavenly techniques and to give us supernatural keys for winning souls to Christ.

After Janet and I learned this new angelic way of soulwinning, we began to put it into practice ourselves. One day, I received a phone call at home from a telemarketer. Generally, I tell telemarketers that I'm not interested in buying anything. However, as I was listening to the woman speak, the Spirit told me to listen to her entire message and then tell her that there are "two kinds of people." I did what the Spirit asked me to do. I waited patiently on the phone, listening to her talk about healthcare, credit-card protection, fitness programs, and long-distance phone plans. Then, at the end of her recitation, she asked me if I had any questions for her. Now I knew that God was setting her up for something great! This was a perfect opportunity to open the door and lead her into the greatest miracle she would ever experience.

I told the woman that, in fact, I *did* have a question: "Did you know that there are only two kinds of nice people who call my house: those who are saved and those who are about to be? Which one are you?" She didn't understand what I was saying, so I repeated myself: "Did you know that there are only two kinds of nice people who call my house: those who are saved and those who are about to be saved? Which one are you?" I had barely finished asking the question for the second time when the woman said, "I'm not saved, and I know that I need Jesus!"

I asked her to repeat this prayer after me: "Father, forgive my sins. Jesus, come into my heart. Make me the kind of person You want me to be. Thank You for saving me." After we finished praying, I asked the woman, "Where is Jesus now?" She responded by saying that Jesus was now in her heart! I told her that she was right and that she could now have a really blessed day.

It's wonderful how creative glory is preparing a way for us to win souls with ease. Because I witnessed to that telemarketer, one more person was added to the kingdom of God. Let the Spirit of God show you creative ways to win souls too.

When I was ministering in Kokomo, Indiana, I had another excellent opportunity to use the same soul-winning technique. As I was getting ready for the meeting one evening, golden glory began to appear all over me, even while I was still in the shower. It was coming up from the pores of my skin and also falling down upon me. I have learned that this special manifestation comes with the supernatural activity of miracle angels. When I experience it, I understand that the Spirit is releasing His glory for a special purpose, and I must be attentive to that purpose. (I will talk further about the manifestation of golden glory in the next chapter.)

As I left my hotel room and began walking down the hallway, I noticed a friendly couple coming toward me. The wife looked at me and said, "You're really sparkling!"

I said, "Yes! This is a miracle from God because Jesus loves you!"

She looked at me again in bewilderment and asked, "But how did it get on you?"

I was so glad that she had asked me another question. Isn't it amazing when God gives us these opportunities to share His love and glory with the world around us? I replied, "Did you know that there are only two kinds of people who ask me that question: those who are saved and those who are about to be? Which one are you?"

She was surprised by my statement and immediately responded, "I guess I'm about to be!" Her husband was glaring at her, wondering what on earth was happening—and it was all happening so quickly!

I took advantage of this opportunity once again. I looked the husband in the eyes and said, "Sir, did you know that there are only two kinds of men who stand in front of me like that: those who are saved and those who are about to be? Which one are you?"

The Spirit must have gripped his heart as I spoke those words because he responded enthusiastically, "I guess I'm about to be too!" Right there, in the hotel hallway, I led this beautiful couple to make a decision for Christ.

After that encounter, I went directly into the conference. That evening, the Lord caused the golden glory to fall and the divine oil to flow in our gathering. It was obvious to us that the angels were moving and ministering in the glory, and even more souls were won to Jesus. Creative glory makes a way!

I have used this soul-winning technique on pizza deliverers, flight attendants, waiters and waitresses, movie theater attendants...and the list goes on! You can be a soulwinner for Christ every single day. Let creative glory lead the way!

SCRIBE ANGELS

Among their various assignments, scribe angels are tasked with keeping written records in heavenly books. They are also given the responsibility of helping believers write the books that they have been mandated by the Spirit to produce. When I am writing, there are times when I can sense an angel standing behind me, helping me to stay focused and on track as I type on my computer keyboard.

Last year, I was "burning the midnight oil" in order to meet a publishing deadline when, suddenly, at a particular moment in the middle of the night, without warning, I knew that I was being surrounded by angels who had come to assist me in my hour of need. I thanked the Lord for sending His angels to help me, and I felt them with me as I worked for the next several hours at my computer, finishing the manuscript that I had been given to write.

The angels' presence was confirmed for me in a unique way when Bill, one of my friends who is a visual artist, felt led that night to send me a picture that he had created specifically for me. It was entitled "Joshua and His Angels." I printed out the picture and hung it on the wall in front of me, giving God the glory for His loving care and concern in sending me heavenly assistance.

I have often felt those angels surrounding me, covering me, and ministering directly to me as I have worked on the books God has laid on my heart to write. Only a writer can fully understand the process involved with taking a book project from its initial concept to final delivery, ready to be received by the world. In the natural, it can be an extremely daunting task. Truth be told, most creative projects impose a great burden upon those who are assigned the responsibility of bringing them to completion. I know this feeling very well, but I have also experienced another kind of feeling when working on my books: the peace and grace of God for writing. I sense it whenever the scribe angels sit down beside me and help me in my efforts.

It is difficult to describe the ways in which God's messengers assist me at such times, but it is a beautiful experience. I've never seen these particular scribe angels, but I feel them when they come. They often seem to arrive after midnight, and they bring with them what we would call "a second wind" of creativity and strength. This is something that many creatives have experienced but have never been able to provide a natural explanation for. That's because it's a divinely supernatural phenomenon! Angels are spirit winds, and when they come, you will experience winds of strength and divine energy being given to you.

Maybe you have felt the presence of creative angels too. When they arrive, you experience a sudden pick-me-up, and then creativity begins to flow. It's as though the atmosphere shifts, and a sudden change occurs. You are able to achieve results much more easily, and your productivity increases because your thoughts are in perfect harmony with creative glory.

One of the reasons angels come into our lives is to help us align properly with the purposes of God in every way. My prayer is that you, too, would experience the heavenly help that comes from scribe angels.

MUSIC ANGELS

The Scriptures say, "*The heavens are telling of the glory of God*" (Psalm 19:1 AMP), and angels are a large part of the celestial body that constantly sings

His praises! We know that angels are involved with music in heaven, but they also want to be involved with the music we create here on earth. Music is the language of the angels.

One of the heavenly messengers that has been assigned to my life is a music angel. He told me his name is Zimri, which, in Hebrew, essentially means "my music, my praise."[30] He is responsible for bringing me new songs. When he comes onto the scene, he brings large scrolls and feeds them to me in the spiritual realm. I know this may sound very unusual, but the Bible records that the prophet Ezekiel and the apostle John received spiritual scrolls to eat. (See Ezekiel 3:1–3; Revelation 10:9.) The scrolls that are given to me are for a much different purpose than those mentioned in the Bible, but they, also, are connected to God's purposes.

When I am leading praise and worship at a service, I can often sense angelic hosts moving into the meeting, and Zimri comes with them, bringing these scrolls. Because of the function of the scrolls, I like to compare them to the old player-piano rolls.

Janet and I recorded our album *Opening the Portals* at Michael W. Smith's home studio in Franklin, Tennessee, which Michael graciously allowed us to use. His son, Tyler, produced the album for us. The studio was a very comfortable and cozy location in which to record, but I was surprised to see that it had old player-piano rolls hanging on its walls. This was such a prophetic moment for me because, whenever I'm singing a new song from the Spirit, it's like I become a player piano. As the music angel brings scrolls from heaven and gives them to me, I play them. I don't have to think about it or try to muster up lyrics in my own ability. I'm not even really consciously thinking about what I'm singing or saying. I receive these songs directly from heaven. I simply open my mouth, and they come out. All I have to do is allow a scroll to unfold, and a song from the Lord comes forth with ease. God is the words and the music. I am only the instrument through which He plays. You, too, can welcome God's angels as they bring new songs, sounds, and melodies with which we can sing God's praises.

ANGELIC IMPARTATION

In the days ahead, expect greater angelic encounters in your life. As you open yourself to receive the fullness of creative glory that has been promised

---

30. For related words, please see https://www.pealim.com/dict/6934-zimra/.

to you, you must be prepared to work with the creative angels God is sending you for the specific tasks He's called you to accomplish. The Spirit desires to fill us with a fresh impartation of creative glory, but we must be open to receive it in the way that He chooses to release it. Let go of any unscriptural mindsets or ideas that would hinder you from partnering with God's angelic host.

Right now, I see angels of creativity coming with golden pens, paintbrushes, musical instruments, and various other tools in their hands. As you look into the spiritual realm, you may see this vision as well. These angels are extending heavenly gifts to you so that you can create in a new way. I also see golden scrolls in their hands, and they are being given to you. In my spirit, I sense that there are new blueprints and plans that God is inviting you to be a part of. Just say yes and receive these gifts. The angels of creativity are ready to help God's people flow in creative glory!

Let's pray together:

Lord, let Your glory come upon us even now and fill us to overflowing. Send the divine supernatural into our midst and give us heavenly solutions for the problems of our day. Thank You for sending Your angels to assist us in fulfilling our callings from You. For our part, we open our hearts and give ourselves to You completely so that You will demonstrate Your creative glory in us and through us. You are leading us in paths of righteousness that are filled with brightness, colors, and sounds that spill out over us with new giftings, talents, and callings. Thank You for allowing us to partner with You and Your angels of creativity. In Jesus's precious and holy name, amen!

CREATIVE GLORY! LET THIS GLORY ARISE IN ME!

PART III:

ENTERING INTO CREATIVE GLORY

A REALM OF CREATIVE MIRACLES

"God did extraordinary miracles through Paul, so that even handkerchiefs and aprons that had touched him were taken to the sick, and their illnesses were cured and the evil spirits left them."
—Acts 19:11–12 (NIV)

We often think of miracles as random occurrences that happen when we least expect them. Although God may perform miracles at any time without notice, there is a supernatural place in the glory realm that we can tap into to discover an unlimited supply of miracles.

One of the gifts of the Spirit mentioned in 1 Corinthians 12:10 is called *"the working of miracles"* (ESV, AMP, KJVER, NKJV). This means that, through the power of the Holy Spirit, we can be given the favor and ability to literally *work* a miracle. I have discovered that creative glory carries the divine instruction needed to work creative miracles. Those who are willing to embrace this instruction and use it for God's glory can receive the power of God to flow in creatively miraculous ways. *Creative glory births creative miracles.*

WHAT IS A CREATIVE MIRACLE?

To define what a creative miracle is, we first need to define the individual words *creative* and *miracle*. The word *creative* means "relating to or involving the imagination or original ideas, especially in the production of an artistic work."[31] The word *miracle* refers to "a surprising and welcome event that is not explicable by natural or scientific laws and is therefore considered to be the work of a divine agency."[32] Thus, a creative miracle is essentially the unexplainable (in human terms) manifestation of the original ideas or imagination of God on earth. This means that when a creative miracle comes to us, it will be given to us directly from God's mind, and it will be something completely original. What an amazing thought!

Remember that the Spirit spoke through the prophet Isaiah, *"For I am about to do something new. See, I have already begun! Do you not see it?"* (Isaiah 43:19 NLT). Some translations, like the *English Standard Version*, use the phrase *"Do you not perceive it?"* When creative glory releases the *new* to us, if we try to figure it out with our natural minds, we may miss the miracle altogether. This is why we need to perceive it with a renewed mind operating in creative glory.

Isaiah continued, *"They are brand new, not things from the past. So you cannot say, 'We knew that all the time!'"* (Isaiah 48:7 NLT). What creative glory is releasing to us in this day is an opportunity to experience the new and never-before-seen miracles of God. Just like the unprecedented manna that fell from heaven for the Israelites in the wilderness, these miracles are flowing to us directly from the open portals of heaven. The new is being poured out upon us, and we may not necessarily have the words or vocabulary to describe its manifestation in detail.

Before she passed on to glory, Ruth Ward Heflin prophesied about this modern-day manna that would be given to us through creative glory:

> I shall do greater things for thee than you have considered. There is glory which is yet to be revealed. You shall not only see it come from the pores of your skin, but you shall see it rain down from the heavenlies. It shall fall from the heavens, even upon the people.
>
> You will be in gatherings where you will see the rain falling inside the building. You will be in meetings where you will see gold dust

---

31. *Lexico*, s.v. "creative," https://www.lexico.com/en/definition/creative.
32. *Lexico*, s.v. "miracle," https://www.lexico.com/en/definition/miracle.

beginning to fall upon the people. I shall do it from within, but I shall also do it from without. I shall do exploits in these last days.

I am working on your faith, for faith must be more than a doctrine. Faith must be an experience day by day, so that when you will see the signs and wonders and miracles I send, you will believe without question.

I am giving you simplicity of faith, and you will walk in it. You will raise the dead. Many of you shall be used in this way also in these last days.

Greater miracles, greater signs and greater wonders are just ahead. Even this day I shall perform miracles for you, My people. I shall do signs among you, I shall do wonders, and I shall do it by My Spirit.

I shall cause an awesome sense of My presence to come into your life, that shall abide with you even from this day forward. And you will walk softly, softly, softly … You will walk softly before Me, and, thus, you will not miss out on what I am doing in the Earth.

—*Thus saith the* LORD![33]

I believe that this prophetic word is for us now more than ever before. By faith, let us move into the fullness of the revelation. Let us capture it in our spirits and allow the Lord to bring it forth in a supernatural way!

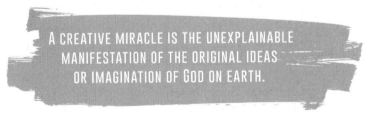

A CREATIVE MIRACLE IS THE UNEXPLAINABLE MANIFESTATION OF THE ORIGINAL IDEAS OR IMAGINATION OF GOD ON EARTH.

GOLDEN GLORY AND THE MIRACULOUS

As I mentioned previously, one of the ways in which God reveals that He is making creative miracles available to us at a particular time is by the sign of golden glory, such as Ruth Heflin prophesied about. On one of my early

---

33. Ruth Ward Heflin, *Golden Glory: The New Wave of Signs and Wonders* (Hagerstown, MD: McDougal Publishing, 2012), 274.

missionary trips to Chennai, India, I witnessed creative glory exhibited in this way. Prophetically speaking, the color gold represents the manifest glory of God and His kingly majesty. In the revival meetings in India, I saw blind eyes opened, deaf ears unstopped, and lame and crippled bodies made whole, along with many other physical healings, signs, wonders, and miracles that only God could do. And, in nearly every service, golden glory "dust" rained down upon us; we could see tiny sparkles of it on our skin and clothing. As a result, in each meeting, many souls were added to the kingdom. Night after night, the altars were filled with people making decisions for Christ. It was a fruitful time of ministry.

UNIQUE OPPORTUNITIES

However, the ministry didn't end when the revival meetings did. On my way back home, as I was traveling through the airport, I had to go through the metal detector at the security checkpoint. I've gone through hundreds of such detectors, and nothing much ever happens. I usually walk right through and go on my way. However, this time, when I went through, the machine began to beep, and the airport security officer asked me to back up and walk through again. When I went through the detector again, it beeped a second time. Once again, I had to move back and then step forward through the detector, and, once again, the machine began to beep.

After this, the officer decided to use a metal wand to see if she could discover where the problem was originating. She asked me to stand on two footprints on the floor. I put my feet on those footprints and stretched my arms out wide, and she proceeded to move the wand around my body—along both of my arms, over and under, then down my sides and across my front and back. Nothing happened until she moved the wand over one of my legs. Suddenly, the wand began to beep! The area that was causing the alarm was around the area of my shin. I was puzzled because I knew I wasn't hiding anything.

The officer asked me to lift my pant leg, and I did as she requested. I was shocked to see a large patch of golden glory covering my lower leg! I couldn't remember ever having golden glory on my leg like that before. Again, this was a huge surprise to me...and a huge surprise to the security guard. She said, "Wow, you're sparkling!"

I said, "Yeah. It's the glory of God. *Jesus did that.*" She asked for my shoes, so I sat down, took off my shoes, and handed them to her. She passed them to another worker, who took them to a separate room for examination. As I was sitting there waiting for my shoes to be returned, I decided to talk more about Jesus to the officer. I understood that India was a Hindu country, and it is against the law to evangelize in public, but when someone asks you a question, you're certainly allowed to answer it. The officer was asking me questions about the golden glory that was covering my shin, so I began talking about Jesus and His miracles and sharing the love of Jesus with her. Isn't that what our faith is all about? The Spirit is sending His creative glory to us so we can have unique opportunities to share the gospel with those who don't yet know the Lord. That's exactly what I was able to do that day in Chennai.

Right there, in the airport security area, I led this woman to Jesus. She bowed her head and repeated the sinner's prayer with me. I believe the Spirit set up that divine appointment. A metal detector had never detected golden glory on me before, and it's never happened since. Creative glory knows how to bring us new opportunities in divine ways.

I believe that the Spirit wants to provide you with opportunities to witness and carry the power of God in your own circle of influence. Such moments may come suddenly, without advance warning, so you must be alert and ready to flow with creative glory!

SIGNS AND WONDERS

When God's glory shows up, it comes with signs and wonders. When you're worshipping the Lord, either privately at home or corporately at church, you may begin to notice tiny flecks of golden or diamond-like dust appearing on the tips of your fingers or on the palms of your hands. (You might even want to check your hands as you read this book.) This golden glory may initially appear very fine, so that it can be detected only as you move your hands back and forth under a light. At other times, it may easily be seen as larger, glitter-like formations. This manifestation comes from God, and we should appreciate it, giving Him the glory.

Jesus is Lord! We mustn't be surprised when the Spirit chooses to give us a sign of gold dust on our hands, for our hands are one of the places where God chooses to release His miraculous power through us to others. This sign represents the miraculous power of God flowing in our lives.[34]

---

34. For more in-depth revelation about God's power flowing through our hands, please see my book *Power Portals* (New Kensington, PA: Whitaker House, 2020).

Still, some people might wonder why God would choose to pour out His golden glory on us. According to the Scriptures, we know that creative glory led King Solomon to build and decorate the temple of God. And this same glory instructed him to overlay the walls with pure gold and ornament the temple with instruments of gold. (See, for example, 1 Kings 6:19–35.) Today, as born-again believers, *we* are the temple of God (see 1 Corinthians 3:16; 6:19), and He chooses to decorate us with the brilliance of His creative glory! Through His glory, we receive a greater anointing for the miraculous.

One time, Janet and I were ministering at a large conference near Scottsdale, Arizona, and a thick golden glory descended on us while we were asleep at the hotel one night. When we woke up the next morning, golden glory dust was on our pillowcases and all over the sheets. We could feel the weighty presence of heaven in our room, and we spontaneously began to worship the Lord. We desired to honor Him for all that He was doing for us.

After a while, I called the front desk and asked, "Would it be possible for us to purchase the bedding in our room?"

The desk clerk seemed surprised and asked, "Why would you want to do that?"

"Well," I said, "heaven moved into our bedroom last night, and our entire bed is covered with gold. We want to take it with us."

"I don't understand what you just said," she replied, "but, yes, you can buy the sheets."

After we purchased the bedding, we carefully wrapped the sheets together; then we took them to the lobby and cut them into small pieces. Why did we do this? We knew that the tangible presence of creative glory could bless many people, and we were determined to distribute each piece of those sheets to someone. When God does a supernatural work, it is always with a purpose. That sign and wonder was to be shared with many other people.

Janet and I took those cloths from the bedding into the next meeting of the conference and gave them to the sick, and many miracles resulted. As we distributed anointed pieces of cloth, just as the early believers did in Acts 19:11–12, multiplied miracles took place.

> WE ARE THE TEMPLE OF GOD,
> AND HE CHOOSES TO DECORATE US WITH THE
> BRILLIANCE OF HIS CREATIVE GLORY!

At times, when we have received a manifestation of heavenly golden glory, God has said that it was a sign of Jesus's soon return. In ancient times, a Jewish bridegroom might send gifts of gold to his bride-to-be while he was away. I believe the Spirit is prophetically telling us that Jesus Christ is coming back very soon.

Other people have told us that, when they have received golden glory, the Lord has shown them a white horse in heaven, pawing restlessly on the golden streets, eager to be on its way. To them, the golden glory is a sign of heaven coming to earth, of the heavenly realm manifesting in our earthly realm. Yes, God wants to fill our lives with heavenly goodness!

But, often, when I have asked the Lord about the appearance of golden glory, He has told me it is a creative sign and wonder, an indicator of creative miracles being present in the spiritual atmosphere. He takes the unseen and makes it seen. He takes the invisible and makes it visible. However, we need to discern the presence of His creative miracles in order to receive them.

God brings heavenly revelation through creative miracles so we can be greater witnesses of His gospel. Let us carry creative glory with us everywhere we go so the world will see that God is all they will ever need.

AN ATMOSPHERE FOR MIRACLES

Many creative miracles occur in an atmosphere of God's glory. I have noted this reality throughout the pages of Scripture, and I have also seen it a number of times in my personal life. I have witnessed miracles of biblical proportions—water turning into wine, the supernatural multiplication of food, the re-creation of people's missing or damaged body parts, and even the creation of new body parts. There are no limitations in creative glory!

How do we help to build an atmosphere of glory? Creative glory comes when we worship the Lord, when we declare God's Word, when we speak by prophetic utterance, and when we sow our finances into the kingdom of God.

These activities create an atmosphere of glory, and where an atmosphere of glory exists, creative miracles are accessible to us.

God's will is that you would have no lack in your spirit, soul, or body; and the way He provides for your needs is through His glory. He wants you to have an abundant overflow of everything you need. This overflow often arrives as creative miracles for those who are open to receive them.

Whatever the Lord shows you, receive it. Cry out to Him, "Lord, I receive it. I receive Your visible creative glory. Speak to me, Holy Spirit. I'm listening. My ears are open. My eyes are open. My heart is open to receive what You are saying."

We can discern an atmosphere for creative miracles not only through golden glory but also through supernatural sound. When I am ministering at a meeting, I can often feel the glory as a vibration in the room, like a hum, as the frequency of the Spirit moves among us. This is the sound of God. If we choose to join in with that sound, we make room to experience His glory in a greater dimension in our own lives and in the lives of those around us.

Other times, I sense God releasing His holy oil to flow in our midst. I feel it falling upon my forehead and running down my cheeks. Then His oil touches my vocal cords and causes them to become anointed instruments of His praise. When we respond to the creative-glory realm, amazing things happen.

I believe God wants to anoint every one of us, in His own way, for His glory. We might each experience creative glory in a distinct way and gain a different perspective on what God is doing in a specific moment. Some people may feel the glory as heat, while others may sense the glory coming as wind. Still others may experience the holy stillness that falls upon a heart that is completely devoted to Him. The particular manifestation of the glory is not what is most important. Just as each one of us is unique in our own right, the Spirit has unique ways of connecting with us heart to heart. He knows what we need, and we must trust His knowledge and wisdom. In whatever way you sense the glory, just know that, in that realm, you are being anointed for miracles.

CREATIVE ARTS AND CREATIVE MIRACLES

As I mentioned earlier in this book, another way creative miracles are manifested is through the arts. God has always intended for the creative arts to be a channel through which His healing can flow. His glory is given to us to allow us to connect with His healing power, and creative glory brings creative healing.

When King Saul suffered from demonic attacks, his aides sought someone who was anointed with music and song to play for the king so that he could be released from this terrible oppression. A shepherd boy named David was able to manifest the heavenly sound that was needed. During the times when he was all alone in the fields with his flocks, David had developed a habit of praising God with his voice and with his musical instrument; as a result, his sound was anointed. David was summoned to the palace, and when he played, sure enough, the evil spirit would lift from King Saul. David carried the sound of creative glory, which is a song of deliverance. He later wrote of the Lord:

> You are my hiding place; you will protect me from trouble and surround
> me with songs of deliverance.   (Psalm 32:7 NIV)

There is such power in the sound of creative glory. But what if that sound is never released? How can it be effective? How can it accomplish what God intends? We must learn how to work miracles through creativity. David learned how to work miracles through music, and I believe that there is a sound in you, too. Release it! Release the deep groanings of the Spirit! Release the sound!

You may be too shy to release it around other people. If this is the case, start alone, where you are—in your bedroom, in the car, or in the shower. The shower is a wonderful place to sing to God. I love it. The reverb of the acoustics is absolutely dynamic. After all, everybody sounds good in the shower. Not everybody sounds good on a CD, but everybody sounds good in the shower! Ha! I've often joked to the sound people in our meetings that increasing the reverb on a microphone will increase the anointing.

There are songs that bring healing and deliverance. Songs can stir up the prophetic flow and cultivate revelation because, in that moment, we become connected with the rhythms of God. The sounds of heaven are never-ending; they are eternally being released. As we tap into the heavenly realm, the sound of glory will cause the unction of the Holy Spirit to flow with insight, supernatural wisdom, and knowledge. Release your creative sounds into the atmosphere!

Remember that, in a sense, God did not create music; God is music. It is part of the essence of who He is. He uses creative glory—with sounds and rhythms and notes and vibrations that resonate—to bring us into His presence. When I am flowing in the Spirit, God is the song that I sing. He is the music that resonates within my soul, the sound that comes out of my mouth. The voice that comes from me is the presence of God; it is part of His very being.

The Lord calls us to make music as we thank and praise Him:

*Enter his gates with thanksgiving and his courts with praise; give thanks
to him and praise his name.* (Psalm 100:4 NIV)

Why must we enter into God's presence with thanksgiving and praise? Because Spirit connects with spirit, and music opens the heavenly door for us as spiritual people, those filled with the Spirit of God.

The Lord gave me a song one afternoon as I was spending time with Him in a hotel room. This song reflects the connection between God's presence, worship, and healing. At first, a little melody went through my spirit. I sang in the Spirit, and then the Lord gave me these words in English:

We come into His presence with our singing.

We come into His healing with our song.

We approach the throne of glory with our voices.

As we seek the Lord, His miracles are known.

Creative glory! Creative glory!

As we seek the Lord, His miracles are known.

Creative glory gives us the ability to sing, dance, or play an instrument as a means to healing. It has been said that the greatest instrument of praise God has given to us is our voice. I agree. But God has also given some of us musical skills on the piano, guitar, drums, or another instrument. You can use any particular instrument to usher creative glory into the atmosphere. (See, for example, 1 Chronicles 25:1–3.)

Creative glory gives an outward expression for an inward impression. In the glory realm, you will begin to hear, see, taste, smell, and feel things. The Spirit gives us an opportunity to share these revelations with others through creative means. But true worship goes much further than just singing a song. True worship is the expression of our devotion to God in every way we can possibly communicate. And through our heartfelt expressions, we are led to experience the miracles of God's glory.

> ## CREATIVE GLORY GIVES AN OUTWARD EXPRESSION FOR AN INWARD IMPRESSION.

For example, it is a biblical concept to take a visual artistic creation and use it in a spiritual way to connect people with God's healing flow. In Numbers 21:8–9, Moses was moved to do this in a very strange way. Jesus later spoke of this event:

Just as Moses lifted up the [bronze] serpent in the desert [on a pole], so must the Son of Man be lifted up [on the cross], so that whoever believes will in Him have eternal life [after physical death, and will actually live forever]. (John 3:14–15 AMP)

At one point on the Israelites' journey from Egypt to the promised land, the people murmured against God and His servant Moses so much that poisonous snakes appeared and bit and killed many of them. God told Moses, "Make a snake and put it up on a pole; anyone who is bitten can look at it and live." That bronze replica of a snake represented Jesus our Healer and the creative flow of God's healing power. Dr. Lisa Harris, chief executive of Eskenazi Health, which is affiliated with the Indiana University School of Medicine, says this about healing and art: "If an art installation gets a patient out of his room or paintings take a person's mind off of their pain and lowers their stress levels, the art isn't just decorative anymore. It's part of the entire model of care."[35]

There are many creative ways in which we can lift up Jesus through the arts. Creative glory exalts Jesus. May God so fill us and flow through us that Christ is lifted up through all that we do. When we are anointed for His glory, whatever we put our hands to will deposit a mark of that glory upon the earth.

---

35. "The Healing Power of Art: Can Hospital Collections Help?" NBC News, September 23, 2014, https://www.nbcnews.com/health/health-news/healing-power-art-can-hospital-collections-help-n208966.

The famous Italian painter, sculptor, architect, and engineer Leonardo da Vinci said, "Where the spirit does not work with the hand, there is no art."[36] True art is a spiritual expression and carries with it an anointing to release creative glory to each observer. This is why, as I wrote earlier, we must be careful what we look at.

What are you observing? What are you paying attention to? Set your mind on the things of glory. Fix your eyes on the things of glory. As you focus on God's glory, let your voice declare His purposes. Let your feet walk in His ways of glory. Let your hands be raised to exalt the Lord Jesus, to praise Him in the glory. God desires His creative glory to flow through you.

I believe that the Lord wants His people in this day to rise up in the arts like never before. He is calling His human creations on earth to carry His glory to new places.

Let the painters paint!

Let the musicians play!

Let the singers sing!

Let the people of God bring forth creative glory on earth!

Lord, thank You that You are moving upon us, stirring something new within us!

Some people may still say, "But Joshua, I don't have that kind of creativity. I don't have the giftings you're talking about." Remember that you are made in the image of your Creator. And the same Spirit who led and directed David, the psalmist; the same Spirit who caused the Israelites to perform and excel in the arts; the same Spirit who flows through the people of God who paint and sing and dance and give God glory—that same Spirit resides inside you.

You have creative glory—claim it!

UNUSUAL OBEDIENCE RELEASES UNUSUAL MIRACLES

To conclude this chapter, I want to reemphasize that receiving creative miracles from the glory realm involves our obedience to God's instructions— even if we don't understand them.

---

36. "Quotable Quote," Goodreads, https://www.goodreads.com/quotes/9696713-where-the-spirit-does-not-work-with-the-hand-there.

CHAIRS FOR THE ANGELS

Several years ago, I was invited to minister in the small town of Wanamingo, Minnesota. I flew to Minneapolis with my best friend, Joshua Fairweather, with whom I have been friends since we were sixteen. Then, we drove about forty-five minutes to our destination. The ministry couple hosting us had rented the local fire hall for our meetings, and we were excited to be there to see all that the Spirit would do.

That afternoon, the Lord spoke to Joshua, telling him to place a chair at the foot of each of our beds in our hotel room. He immediately obeyed without questioning the Lord. Afterward, when he asked God about it, the Lord told him, "They are for your angels."

We didn't see any angels, and we didn't sense the presence of any angels, but we decided to pray about this revelation to see what God was saying to us. I remembered the biblical reference to the angel that would come down once a year to stir the water in the Pool of Bethesda in Jerusalem. In my mind, I could visualize that angel with a big staff in his hand, stirring up the water, making it healing water. Whoever first stepped into the water at the moment it was stirred would be healed. Those otherwise natural waters became miracle waters. (See John 5:1–4 AMP, KJVER, NKJV.)

The miracle angel that was standing in the Pool of Bethesda had creative glory in his hands. No wonder that water got stirred up! No wonder it became healing water! No wonder creative miracles were released there! And God is ready to loose angels of creative glory in your life too. God's angels love His presence and spend much of their time simply basking in the atmosphere of creative glory. Then, when they are directed toward earth and released to bless our lives, they come with the creativity of heaven.

Remember, creative glory has the ability to release much more than healing. It can release all kinds of creative miracles in your life, in the lives of your family members, at your workplace, in your community, anywhere. Creative miracles can be released whenever creative glory arrives on the scene.

When I was growing up, my cousins and I would visit our grandmother for a week every summer. Before bedtime, we would all get up in Grandmother's bed, and she would read to us from one of her books about the Spirit-filled life. In one of those books, the author related how, as a young boy, he had been caught up into the heavenly realm, and the experience had captured his heart. That story also captured my heart; I have never forgotten it. In heaven, the boy saw a building that looked like a warehouse filled with spare body parts, arranged in an orderly way on shelves. There were arms, legs, hearts, lungs, and every other kind of body part. When the boy asked God about what he had seen, he was told that this was what was available to the people of God. When they pressed in for creative miracles, God would send the needed body part from heaven to earth. As I mentioned previously, I have seen the manifestation of that reality many times. When I am praying, I often suddenly see something supernatural coming from the heavenly realm to the earthly realm.

I am convinced that when the angel stirred the water of the Pool of Bethesda, those extra body parts were made available to anyone who needed them and pressed in to receive them. That is why, when my friend Joshua set the chairs at the foot of our beds for the angels, I knew that two of God's messengers had been sent to stir up healing waters for us so that we could minister to the people at the meeting.

STIRRING THE WATER

That night, when I stood behind the pulpit in the fire hall in Minnesota, I felt the presence of the angels and was convinced they were there to stir up the water. I also knew that, in front of me, in the altar area that had been set up, there was a spiritual Pool of Bethesda. In the natural, I did not see anything, but in the glory realm, I could see and sense God's healing provision. I gave voice to that prophetic revelation, declaring what God was doing for His people.

Don't wait until you physically see a change to say that something is changing. When God reveals something to you in the glory realm, that's the time to speak it. Open your mouth and declare it, proclaim it, command it, decree it! Speak it out boldly because what He shows you in the glory is what He is offering for you to receive in the natural. Take hold of it by faith and, through the Spirit's anointing, pull it down. Draw on creative glory. As you speak out Spirit-inspired words with a powerful anointing, realms of glory will manifest in the atmosphere around you.

When I announced that there was a Pool of Bethesda coming into the altar area, the creative glory of God manifested in that place. What I was seeing in the Spirit realm happened in the physical world. A woman who had a lump on her breast went into the healing pool as the water was being stirred by the angels. When she stepped into that flow, the lump instantly disappeared.

Many other wonderful miracles happened. People who were lame and had other debilitating issues with their bodies got up out of their seats and surged forward toward the invisible pool filled with Spirit-stirred water. One man was suffering terribly from knee pain. The joints were bone on bone, making it difficult for him to walk. He went haltingly into the pool, but he came out running on the other side! He ran around the hall and then kept running in circles. He later testified that he believed new cartilage had been miraculously inserted into his knees. His joints no longer felt like they were bone on bone. He had no pain, and he now walked—and ran—with ease. What had happened? God's creative glory had released a creative miracle.

WHAT GOD SHOWS YOU IN THE GLORY IS WHAT HE IS OFFERING FOR YOU TO RECEIVE IN THE NATURAL!

SUPERNATURAL TRANSFORMATION

When Joshua and I returned to our hotel room that night, we were on such a spiritual high that there was no way we were going to be able to sleep. All we could think about were the miracles we had seen, the glory that had flowed, and the angels that had done their work of stirring up the water. How could we sleep when we kept remembering the goodness of God and His holy presence?

This wasn't the first time I'd had difficulty falling asleep after an evening of miraculous ministry. Over time, I had tried various methods to help me sleep, and I had discovered that if I turned on a boring television program, I would soon be in a deep sleep. That night, I turned on the TV in the hotel room, but instead of seeing a boring program, I saw a very anointed preacher who was talking about the power of communion. What he was saying was awesome, and deep revelation was flowing. I didn't want to miss a word, but I was thirsty, so I asked Joshua, who was in the bathroom brushing his teeth, if he would bring me some water in a plastic cup. I took a couple of sips and didn't notice anything unusual about the water. But when I took a third sip, I realized that something had changed. What was now in the cup was very different from water.

When the Lord told Joshua to put the chairs at the ends of our beds and then revealed they were for angels that were going to stir up healing water, I had no idea that God's messengers also had another assignment. I looked into that plastic cup, and the water had supernaturally become a heavenly wine!

When Joshua saw what had happened to the water, he nearly swallowed his toothbrush. We started laughing, then crying, then laughing again! We were so touched by the presence of God and what had just happened! Angels had stirred the water and turned it into miracle wine. Remarkable!

Why would God do that? Well, the minister we were listening to on TV was preparing to serve communion; and, supernaturally, the Spirit provided us with the communion wine. In that moment, we wondered, "Will the Lord rain down manna as He did in the wilderness?" That didn't happen, but we did have a bagel left over from breakfast that we used for our communion bread. We had the miracle wine for our communion drink, and we shared the body and blood of Jesus with our brothers and sisters in Christ.

A message with a phone number was scrolling across the bottom of the TV screen, encouraging anyone who had a testimony to call. We were now so drunk in the Spirit that we called and told the person who answered that God had just turned water into wine for us. I'm not sure our testimony was believed, but it was true. God's glory had provided a creative miracle to encourage us and bring honor to His name.

Was what happened to us scriptural? Of course it was. In Jesus's day, creative glory released creative miracles. The very first recorded miracle Jesus did was to turn water into wine at a marriage feast in Cana of Galilee. (See John 2.) The Scriptures record that, when this wine was brought forth, the master of ceremonies was amazed:

> When the master of ceremonies tasted the water that was now wine, not knowing where it had come from (though, of course, the servants knew), he called the bridegroom over. "A host always serves the best wine first," he

said. "Then, when everyone has had a lot to drink, he brings out the less expensive wine. But you have kept the best until now!"

(John 2:9–10 NLT)

The new wine of the Spirit is flowing, and God offers only the very best. *"Taste and see that the LORD is good!"* (Psalm 34:8 ESV).

After hearing the account of how the angel turned my water into wine, many people ask me, "Was the wine you received alcoholic?" Here is my response: Everything that God gives us is alive. It is vibrant. There is no death in Him. But in order to make alcohol, something has to die and ferment. When you have the wine of the Holy Spirit in your glass, and you drink it, you get better than drunk: you drink in everlasting life, the most superior drink you could ever hope to swallow in this life on earth.

The wine of the Spirit is vibrant and filled with light, joy, peace, and everything good that comes from Him. It is creative glory in a cup. Can *you* experience this vibrancy too? Absolutely! Just put your hands out in front of you and say, "Father, in the name of Jesus, I invite You to fill me up. I give You my water, and I ask You to turn it into heavenly wine. I give You what I have, asking You to stir it up, rearrange it, and transform it into what You want it to be. May all that remains be heavenly and glorious and miraculous. I pray all this in Jesus's mighty name. Amen."

I believe that waters are being supernaturally stirred within you even now. As you feel the heavenly glory, you may sense a vibration or something stirring in you. You may experience what feels like an electrical frequency passing through your body. It might come as waves, moving or rippling up and down your body. Whatever you feel, just yield to the realm of God. Yield to the Holy Spirit being released to you right now. Yield to God's transformational process, the work of His creative glory birthing something new in you.

The Cana wedding scene ends with these words:

This, the first of his signs, Jesus did at Cana in Galilee, and manifested his glory. And his disciples believed in him. (John 2:11 ESV)

When God introduces us to the realm of creative glory, He releases creative miracles in our midst. We see physical changes in our atmosphere, we feel physical changes within our own bodies, and we notice changes within our family members and in our communities. We also see changes within our particular realms of provision, including our finances. As the Lord of Glory manifests creative glory, the sign will be the creative miracles He releases.

CREATIVE GLORY! LET THIS GLORY ARISE IN ME!

9

WORKING CREATIVE MIRACLES

"A vast crowd brought to him people who were lame, blind, crippled,
those who couldn't speak, and many others. They laid them before
Jesus, and he healed them all."
—Matthew 15:30 (NLT)

There is no right or wrong way to work a miracle when you're being led by the Spirit. Let God show you new and exciting ways to cooperate with Him to see His power released in your life and in the lives of those around you. Remember, God wants to do something unique as He demonstrates His glory and love through you.

CREATIVE MIRACLES IN JESUS'S MINISTRY

During the three-year period that Jesus worked miracles when He walked on earth as a human being, He released the Spirit's power in a variety of ways. Let's review several examples, some of which we will look at in more depth in this chapter.

- Jesus fed thousands of people with five loaves of bread and two fish by giving thanks to God and then breaking the food into pieces and distributing it. (See, for example, Matthew 14:15–21.)

- Jesus laid His anointed hands upon the sick, and they miraculously recovered through His touch. (See, for example, Luke 13:10–13.)

- Jesus allowed the sick to lay their hands upon Him, and healing virtue flowed from Him with miraculous power. (See, for example, Luke 8:43–48.)

- Jesus walked on water by faith and invited Peter to do the same—and he did. (See Matthew 14:22–33.)

- Jesus raised His friend Lazarus from the dead by praying to the Father and then calling Lazarus forth from the tomb. (See John 11:38–44.)

- Jesus created wedding wine by filling ceremonial jars with water. (See John 2:1–11.)

- Jesus miraculously cured blindness by spitting in the dirt, creating mud, and then placing it on a blind man's eyes. (See John 9:1–11.)

- Jesus, not confined by distance, spoke a healing word and sent it forth to work a healing miracle. (See, for example, Matthew 8:5–13.)

We can discover many other examples of creative miracles within the Gospels, and this leads me to believe that there are many more and varied ways in which the Spirit desires to creatively work miracles through us. We must do the works of Him who sends us. (See John 9:4.) After all, Jesus said:

I assure you and most solemnly say to you, anyone who believes in Me [as Savior] will also do the things that I do; and he will do even greater things than these [in extent and outreach], because I am going to the Father.

(John 14:12 AMP)

The most important thing to remember is that what works for others may not always work for you. This is a major reason why you must follow the leading of creative glory. Doing so releases you from a performance mentality and the "demands of man," and it grants you the freedom to simply flow in the Spirit.

UNIQUE HEALING OINTMENTS

As I mentioned above, guided by the Spirit, Jesus employed various unusual methods when performing miracles. Let's take a closer look at one classic biblical example of this:

> As Jesus was walking along, he saw a man who had been blind from birth. "Rabbi," his disciples asked him, "why was this man born blind? Was it because of his own sins or his parents' sins?" "It was not because of his sins or his parents' sins," Jesus answered. "This happened so the power of God could be seen in him. We must quickly carry out the tasks assigned us by the one who sent us. The night is coming, and then no one can work. But while I am here in the world, I am the light of the world." Then he spit on the ground, made mud with the saliva, and spread the mud over the blind man's eyes. He told him, "Go wash yourself in the pool of Siloam" (Siloam means "sent"). So the man went and washed and came back seeing!
>
> (John 9:1–7 NLT)

It is interesting to note that Jesus's disciples, influenced by a spirit of religion, tried to point a finger of accusation at either the man or his parents: Why was this man blind? What had he or his parents done to cause his affliction? Were they involved in sinful activities or relationships? Jesus's answer was very gracious: "It was not because of his sins or his parents' sins.... This happened so the power of God could be seen in him." Jesus went on to declare that He must work now, in the daylight.

What Jesus was saying is that it was not the time to point fingers at anyone, not the time for blaming or bickering about why the man was blind. When there is sickness, disease, famine—a serious problem of any kind—Jesus wants to be revealed in that situation. He wants us to see His glory in the midst of anything that looks terrible in the natural.

Jesus proceeded to spit on the ground, mix up some mud with the spit, and then anoint the eyes of the blind man. That was indeed an unusual thing to do. Then Jesus said to the man, "Go wash yourself in the pool of Siloam." The result of the man's obedience was that he "came back seeing!" His healing immediately caused a great stir in the neighborhood:

His neighbors and others who knew him as a blind beggar asked each other, "Isn't this the man who used to sit and beg?" Some said he was, and others said, "No, he just looks like him!" But the beggar kept saying, "Yes, I am the same one!" They asked, "Who healed you? What happened?" He told them, "The man they call Jesus made mud and spread it over my eyes and told me, 'Go to the pool of Siloam and wash yourself.' So I went and washed, and now I can see!" (John 9:8–11 NLT)

What a wonderful testimony of God's provision for healing! I love this story because Jesus healed the man in such a creative way, making mud from spit and dirt to use as a healing ointment. Jesus received the revelation to do this from the Father, and the results were miraculous.

When Jesus heals, He always does so in a creative way. That is why, if we want to bring healing to the world around us, we need to enter into creative glory. Sometimes we are so busy with our routines and traditions that we don't seek what the Spirit wants to give us—and thus we don't receive the heavenly results we need or desire. At times, we are so busy trying to imitate or duplicate what someone else has done that we miss our healing miracle altogether. God has something unique for each of us. He has a creative flow that He designed specifically for us.

One time, God led me to use a unique form of healing ointment too. Several years ago, I had just finished a series of revival meetings at a church in Texas, and a middle-aged woman approached me when I walked out to my car in the church parking lot. She had been suffering from a sickness and had come to the revival meetings desperate for a miracle. She proceeded to tell me, "I saw a vision of you anointing my head with supernatural oil, and when you did, I was totally healed." I was glad that she had so much faith to believe that a miracle was possible. The only problem was that I didn't have any oil available to anoint her with, let alone *supernatural* oil. At least, I didn't think I did. I was standing in front of my car, and I was prepared to tell her that I wasn't able to do what she had requested, when suddenly the voice of the Spirit began speaking to my heart. The instruction I received surprised me because I had never considered it before. The Spirit told me, "Lift the hood of your car, take oil from the dipstick, and anoint her head."

I pondered this message, thinking, "If the ancients could use olive oil for anointing, why couldn't the moderns use motor oil for the same purpose? If

God wants to bless it, He can." In that moment, my options were either to ignore the voice or follow the heavenly guidance I had received. I chose to do the latter. The instruction was unusual, and it was creative, but that is often the way the Spirit releases miracles through us. He gives us a special prompting in our hearts directly from Him.

My friend Debbie Kendrick shared this advice with me: "The highest way God can lead us is by desire. In the glory, He floats the desires of His heart into ours. We can trust our hearts because they have been redeemed, tried, and tested." Let your heart lead you by desire in the realms of creative glory.

As I followed this creative-glory instruction by wiping my hands on the dipstick and anointing the woman's head with the greasy and seemingly dirty substance, I witnessed miraculous results. That ordinary motor oil became a supernatural point of contact for God to do great things. Just as the woman had seen in her vision, when I anointed her with oil that God infused with supernatural power, she received a complete and total healing within her body. All glory to God!

CREATIVE TECHNIQUES

Let's look at a few more examples of the creative techniques Jesus used as He was prompted by the Spirit. In John 11, Jesus used His voice to call His friend Lazarus out of the grave.

> "Roll the stone aside," Jesus told them. But Martha, the dead man's sister, protested, "Lord, he has been dead for four days. The smell will be terrible." Jesus responded, "Didn't I tell you that you would see God's glory if you believe?" So they rolled the stone aside. Then Jesus looked up to heaven and said, "Father, thank you for hearing me. You always hear me, but I said it out loud for the sake of all these people standing here, so that they will believe you sent me." Then Jesus shouted, "Lazarus, come out!" And the dead man came out, his hands and feet bound in graveclothes, his face wrapped in a headcloth. Jesus told them, "Unwrap him and let him go!"
> (John 11:39–44 NLT)

Jesus didn't go in to where Lazarus was influenced and pull him out of the tomb with His hands. He just called His friend's name, and Lazarus's dead body came to life. Lazarus responded to Jesus's call by walking out of the tomb, alive and well!

In another instance, Jesus commanded a group of demons to come out of a man. But Jesus didn't stop there. He then allowed the wild, evil spirits to go into a herd of pigs that immediately ran down the mountainside and drowned themselves in the sea. What a dramatic and justified ending to the oppression of those evil spirits! (See Luke 8:26–36.)

In Luke 17, Jesus healed a group of ten lepers from a distance by telling them to go and be inspected by the priests. (Being inspected by a priest was a requirement of the law for full cleansing from leprosy; see Leviticus 14:1–32.) As the Son of God, He could have healed the men by approaching them and touching them with His anointed hands, as He had done for others who were ill. (See, for example, Matthew 8:1–4; Luke 4:40.) Instead, He chose to follow the flow of heaven, the flow of creative glory, and give them a specific instruction from the Spirit to obey. (See Luke 17:11–19.)

We must always remember that Jesus didn't just do whatever He wanted to do. He declared,

> Truly, truly, I say to you, the Son can do nothing of his own accord, but only what he sees the Father doing. For whatever the Father does, that the Son does likewise.   (John 5:19 ESV)

If you and I want to enter into the creative-glory realm, we, too, must be willing to look into heaven and see what the Father is doing.

CREATIVE PRAYERS

We know that our Spirit-led prayers are an integral part of bringing God's healing and miracles to others. And God wants to use creative glory even in our intercession. Many years ago, Janet and I were led by creative glory into a new way of praying for the people of the world: we discovered that we could dance in the Spirit over the maps of nations, claiming those countries for God. Whether in the privacy of our own bedroom, at the altar of a church or tabernacle, or wherever we were, we could ask God for nations, and He would give them to us. Janet and I began to put this wonderful revelation into practice for specific geographical locations, believing for those regions to learn and partake of God's salvation. On one occasion, I spread out a map of California on the floor of our living room and danced all over it. We had been seeing reports in the news about a severe drought, and several people had reached out to us asking if we would pray about the situation. Some of the greatest intercession can be done in a creative way as we allow the Spirit of God to lead us. As we danced over the map, we sang about the rain, we prophesied rain, and, in the Spirit realm, we were "dancing in the rain." A few days later, the natural manifestation appeared as rain began to fall in California. God brings supernatural answers to our prayers through creative glory.

You can do the same thing for your spouse, siblings, children, grandchildren, coworkers, or anyone else God places on your mind and heart. Bring photos of your loved ones or other people who are in need into your place of worship and intercession. Hold up the photos before God or dance over them. God wants to do great miracles for us, but it takes spiritual people to release heaven's desires. This is the working of creative glory!

Stop concentrating on how long your family members have been running from God or how rebellious they have been. Believe for God's will to be done for them in the glory; declare the promises of God over them, and change will happen. God gives us creative glory to bring forth His unique solutions for our difficulties.

> IT TAKES SPIRITUAL PEOPLE TO RELEASE HEAVEN'S DESIRES.

CREATIVE WORSHIP

Let's never forget that healing through creative glory is available not only for those around us, but also for us personally. And, often, the realms of creative glory will open up to us through our faith-filled worship. A few years ago, I was invited to minister in Taiwan, and something very unusual happened to me. I was to teach a Glory School in Taipei, as I had done several years in a row. Ministers came to this event from all over Taiwan, as well as Hong Kong, Singapore, Mainland China, and other countries. At this Glory School, there were about four hundred leaders in attendance, representing thousands of believers. Some pastors had hundreds of churches under their leadership. It was a great honor to be with them, and I was looking forward to it.

I arrived in Taipei after a long flight and discovered that the meeting host had arranged for me to stay at one of the most beautiful and extravagant hotels in Taipei—the Grand Hotel, which is indeed *grand*. The lobby is about the size of a football field, stretching from one end of the mammoth building to the other, and is lavishly decorated with ornate furnishings: marble floors; stunning, giant red columns; and huge floral displays. My suite was equally impressive and was a wonderful place to stay during my ministry there.

I was very excited about the message I was going to bring to God's people gathered in that city. The time for the meeting came, and I was preparing to leave my room when, suddenly, I was unable to move my right leg. It was completely stiff. The joints in my hip and knee were locked in place. This had never happened to me before, and I wasn't sure exactly what had caused it. No matter what I tried, my leg refused to loosen.

I knew that one of my hosts was waiting for me downstairs, and I had to get to the meeting. What should I do? Taiwan was the first stop on a five-nation tour of Asia I had planned. How could I minister all that time with a right leg that wasn't working? "Jesus," I prayed, "You need to help me, please."

After a little while, I grabbed my Bible. Then, dragging my leg behind me, I slowly made my way down the long hall, onto the elevator, and into the lobby. As I shuffled all the way across that enormous space to meet my host, I tried to disguise the fact that my leg was not working properly. I didn't want them to see me struggling to walk because I didn't know how to explain what had happened or why.

I finally reached the front doors, met my host, and hobbled to the car waiting for me outside. I silently prayed, "Lord, I have never been in this auditorium and don't know how it is arranged, but You do. Please let me preach down on the main floor, as close to my seat as possible."

After the short ride to the meeting venue, I struggled to walk into the huge auditorium. My heart sank when I saw the platform: it was one of the highest stages I had ever seen! There was a staircase on either side. I would have to climb up all those steps when it was time for me to minister. How I was going to do that, I wasn't at all sure.

During the worship time, I stood up and tried to move my hip and bend my knee, but they remained rigid. I pondered, "How can I get up onto that platform without everybody seeing my serious problem?" I thought and thought. Finally, it came to me. When it was my turn, the pastor handed me the microphone at my seat, and I said to the crowd, "Raise your hands to heaven, close your eyes, and worship the Lord." While everyone's eyes were closed, I pulled my leg into position and dragged it with me up the stairs and to the middle of the platform. I preached the whole evening from that one spot, never moving. God did many miracles for other people that night, but I continued to suffer from a leg that refused to respond.

I have heard people say, "If Kathryn Kuhlman was such a miracle healer, why did she herself have to deal with sickness?" I know that healing doesn't come to us because of our own merits. It comes to us because of the finished work of Jesus Christ on the cross of Calvary. Jesus bore the stripes on His back so that we could be healed, and it's up to us to live in that healing provision every day of our lives. We don't receive special privileges because of anything we have done. It's all about Him.

So, why was I suffering that evening? What happened to me was obviously a direct attack of the enemy, and there are many things I don't fully understand about what happened. But I choose to focus on the truth I *do* know: God's desire is always to heal. He wants to heal us every time we need His touch. No matter what you are going through, that is the first important truth you must remember.

During that situation, if I had focused on the questions surrounding my frozen-leg experience, it could have led me to despair or doubt. But I knew that if I focused on the truth, I would find the healing I needed. My circumstances would have to change; they would have to line up with God's healing promises.

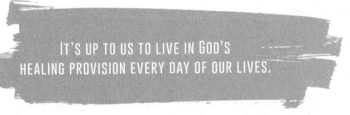

IT'S UP TO US TO LIVE IN GOD'S HEALING PROVISION EVERY DAY OF OUR LIVES.

When I returned to my hotel room that night, I was very upset with the enemy. Again, I recognized that there was no way I could minister in five Asian cities with a completely stiff leg. As I sat in my room, frustrated about the demonic assignment that was waging war against my physical health, the Lord spoke to my spirit. What He said to me that night was a reminder of what He had spoken to me many years before. He told me, "Joshua, with every new day comes a new song, and with every new song comes a new realm of glory."

I thought, "Okay, I just need to sing over this. I just need to find my new song." It was already late at night, but, suddenly, a very light and airy tune vibrated in my spirit. I was picking up on some heavenly frequencies, some glory vibrations. I heard the sound, and then I began to hum it. Soon, I had a melody. I suddenly knew what I needed to do with that melody. As Paul wrote,

> *I will pray with the spirit, and I will pray with the understanding also: I will sing with the spirit, and I will sing with the understanding also.*
> (1 Corinthians 14:15 KJVER)

If I wanted to understand this heavenly song, I would first have to pray and sing in the Spirit. And that's what I did. I sang in the Spirit the melody God had placed in my heart, and, at the same time, I dragged my leg around the room. I forced my leg to move. Why did I do that? I understood that if I wanted healing in my leg, I had to walk because that's what legs do. My leg was made for walking, so, in order to realize the healing I knew God desired for me to have, I had to *work the miracle* in faith. Therefore, as I sang in the Spirit, I pulled my leg around the room, demanding that it move in all directions.

BELIEVE THE TRUTH OF GOD ABOUT YOUR SITUATION AND MOVE INTO THAT TRUTH!

The enemy will try many ways to block you from receiving healing. He doesn't want you to have the best that God has for you. But don't believe his lies. Refuse to come into agreement with the curse. Instead, come into agreement with the blessings of the heavenlies. Believe God's truth about your situation, and move into that truth. The Bible tells us,

The kingdom of heaven suffers violence, and the violent take it by force.
(Matthew 11:12 KJVER)

Some miracles come by "force." Creative glory brings us the strength and courage to boldly receive them. I'm referring to standing strong by faith, grabbing hold of the Word of God, and declaring, "This is my realm. This is my territory. God's creative glory has provided healing for me."

The enemy spirit never plays fair. He is the father of lies, and he is terribly violent. (See John 8:44.) He attacks us viciously and throws every conceivable deception our way. That is why we must use the full force of our faith against him.

As I continued singing in the Spirit, eventually, this new song began coming to me in words I could understand:

The glory of God is working in me, working in me.

The glory of God is working in me, working in me.

As I walk this walk of faith,

Each and every step I take,

The glory of God is working in me, working in me.

Then, suddenly, the glory came and hit me, instantly freeing my knee and unlocking my hip! I moved and danced all around that room as I kept singing:

The glory of God is working in me, working in me.

The glory of God is working in me, working in me.

As I walk this walk of faith,

Each and every step I take,

The glory of God is working in me, working in me.

My faith had become my reality!

When God's glory gets into your soul, He will give you a new song, and you may wake up in the night singing that song. It will stick with you for a while, and you'll think of it throughout the day. When you get into the glory, and the glory gets into you, go with the flow. Go to sleep singing the Spirit's song and wake up singing that song. Whatever He gives you in the glory is for your advantage.

God's creative glory brought me much-needed release through a spiritual song from the glory realm. Sometimes, we need to sing and dance in our healing, giving God praise. We need to move in the glory, believing for the solutions to our needs and the needs of our family members. We can pray, "Lord, let Your creative glory come with a release of miracles, with a download of Your power. Direct our paths and cause us to move in the places where You are leading us. Cause our every step to be in tune with Your Spirit."

Having a working leg was important to the Asian ministry tour God had called me to. Likewise, your legs and feet may be especially important to your present and future ministry for the Lord. Let God touch them for His glory. The Scriptures say, "*How beautiful are the feet of those who bring good news of good things!*" (Romans 10:15 AMP; see also Isaiah 52:7). You are to be a spiritual walker, and every place your feet tread, God will give to you for His glory and your benefit. May your beautiful feet be blessed with creative glory this day, and all foot and leg problems be healed so that you can realize your glorious future.

Move your feet today. Dance before the Lord, and let His healing glory come upon you in a creative flow of the Spirit. Healing comes in the glory. Test it and see what God has done for you. Your case is not too hard for Him. Nothing is impossible with Him. Believe it and act on His promise today. As you do, the glory of God will be upon your legs and feet.

We don't come to our God, the Almighty, just to see what we can get from Him. We come to honor, praise, and worship Him because of who He is. But when you get into His presence, it is impossible to leave in the same condition in which you came. When you are in the presence of almighty God, you touch the realms of creative glory—the realm of provision, the realm of healing, the realm of miracles—where there is always something new for you.

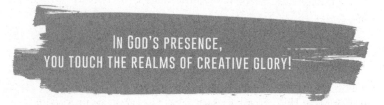

IN GOD'S PRESENCE,
YOU TOUCH THE REALMS OF CREATIVE GLORY!

HEARING GOD'S CREATIVE INSTRUCTIONS

I emphasized earlier that, in order to move in creative miracles, we first need to hear the Father's voice and follow His instructions, just as Jesus did. And we must learn to recognize when He is speaking to us. The Spirit demonstrated this truth for me in an unexpected way. For several days, I had suffered from a painful area at the back of my mouth. I was trusting God that it would get better, but it became worse until I finally made an appointment with my dentist.

After examining me and taking an X-ray, he said, "Your wisdom teeth are impacted, which is quite common. They need to be extracted, and it will take you a few days to recover. Otherwise, the problem should be resolved."

I didn't like the sound of that recovery period. I had a full ministry schedule and places where I needed to be. "I'm not sure when I can do it," I told him. "My calendar is so full."

"Well, the sooner the better," he said. "When you find something you can cancel, call the office and make an appointment. This can be very serious, so I wouldn't put it off for too long, or you'll be sorry."

Back home, I continued to experience pain, and it was getting progressively worse, so I called the pastor who was coordinating a conference where I was scheduled to minister the next weekend. I explained the situation and asked to be excused from my commitment. However, arrangements were made for Janet and another minister to take my place at that conference.

I called the dentist's office, and when the surgery was scheduled, the assistant gave me very specific instructions: "Make sure you do *not* eat anything at all after midnight on the night before the surgery. But do drink lots of water because we're in the desert, and you don't want to get dehydrated."

I did as I was told. I ate nothing after midnight the night before the surgery and had no breakfast before I went to our ministry office in the morning. Remembering what the assistant had said about drinking lots of water, I drank all the water we had at the office. But that didn't seem like enough, so I went to a nearby store and bought a small case of water and drank every bottle.

When it came time to leave for the surgery, I was feeling very full of water, and I thought that must be good. I was ready for the procedure.

At the dentist's office, the assistant checked me in and said, "You didn't eat after midnight, right?"

"No, I didn't eat anything after midnight," I answered.

"And you haven't had anything to drink either, right?" she asked.

Startled, I answered, "What? I actually drank A LOT of water. I thought you told me to drink water."

"Oh, no! No, you should never drink before surgery."

I said, "I did. I drank."

"When was the last time you drank anything?"

"About ten minutes ago."

"Well, it's probably okay. How much did you drink?"

"I drank an entire case of water. I think it was twelve bottles."

At this point, the dentist, who was in a back room, overheard our conversation and came wheeling out into the hall on a chair with rollers. He looked down the hallway and said, "I'm not doing the surgery."

The assistant was very upset with me. "I told you not to drink water."

I replied, "But I heard you very specifically tell me to drink lots of water because we're in the desert, and I shouldn't get dehydrated."

"I would never tell somebody something like that," she insisted.

I didn't say it, but I was thinking to myself, "That's exactly what I heard you say."

Then I remembered that Jesus said He only did what He saw the Father doing and only said what He heard the Father saying. Maybe I just thought I was hearing the assistant when, in reality, I was hearing from God Himself.

Many times, people have told me that they had really needed something I said at a service. When I asked which words had touched them, they told me something that I was sure I hadn't said at all. I believe that while I was preaching, they had heard from God Himself.

There are times when God intervenes in a moment of divine revelation and tells us something we especially need to hear. We think we're hearing a person, but it's really God. If we obey what we have heard the Lord say in this unusual way, we enter into a realm of the divine supernatural. In my case, it was the realm of divine healing.

Because I had consumed so much water, my surgery was canceled and rescheduled for a few days later. But when I returned home that afternoon, the pain had decreased significantly. I decided that if drinking a lot of water could cause it to improve that much, I would drink even more water for the rest of the day, and I did. The next morning, when I woke up, I had absolutely no pain in my mouth. The day after that, there was still no pain.

I called the dentist's office and canceled the surgery. "I don't need it now," I told them. "I'm not having any pain at all."

"Well, your wisdom teeth are still going to bother you," they told me. "You really need to get them taken care of."

I want to report that this happened thirteen years ago! And from that time until now, I have not had any pain in my mouth, and I still have my wisdom teeth. God performed a creative healing, and I give Him all the glory. I was even able to go to the second half of that conference to minister!

MAY GOD'S HEALING GLORY COME UPON YOU IN A CREATIVE FLOW OF THE SPIRIT!

Am I saying that if you have pain in your mouth, you should drink twelve bottles of water? No! It worked for me, but it may not work for you. The key is not drinking more water. The key is listening to the creative instruction of God, allowing creative glory to come to you and show you what is needed for that particular moment.

As I said, sometimes God lets us hear what we need to hear instead of what is actually being said. This is how creative glory works. It gives us the supernatural tools we need to connect with Jesus Christ, our Healer. Creative glory is a seed, and wholeness is the fruit of its growth and development.

CREATIVE GLORY! LET THIS GLORY ARISE IN ME!

10

CREATIVE CONNECTIONS

"Set your mind and keep focused habitually on the things above
[the heavenly things], not on things that are on the earth
[which have only temporal value]."
—Colossians 3:2 (AMP)

Recently, in the Spirit realm, I saw a vision of extraordinary places that I call "creative-glory hubs." It was a visual depiction of the way in which creative people connect spiritually as God brings them together for His purposes. Each glory hub looked like a wheel with a large, spinning outer rim; various spokes that looked like tubes; and a pulsating hub in the center of them (like the wheel within a wheel from Ezekiel's vision in Ezekiel 1:15–21). The hub in the middle was the faith-core; it was filled with God's divine energy because that is where creatives come together. This hub was fully inclusive—connecting people old and young, of all ethnicities and backgrounds, with a variety of abilities, all flowing together in unity and oneness in the Lord.

The various spokes represented the many different avenues through which creativity can be released into the world—the visual arts, music, innovations, movement, performance art, design, social media, publishing, engineering, and many more—each having its own channel of expression. Great power flowed like oil through these spokes, moving down the tubes and into the outer rim. This flow caused a synergy that was electrifying! As the outer rim was spinning around and around, being charged by the various creative expressions, supernatural lightning was released from the wheels, impacting the atmosphere around them. It was the glory being manifested! The wheels were advancing—again, similar to the wheels that Ezekiel saw moving because *"the spirit of the living creatures was in the wheels"* (Ezekiel 1:20 ESV, NIV, NKJV).

The hub in the center of the wheel was filled with unity because that's the place where creatives gather together. Spirit-filled creatives carry the very nature of God, as reflected in the appearance of the living creatures Ezekiel described: while we function in the creative anointing given to humankind, we're as bold and ferocious as a lion, as humble and willing to serve God's purposes as an ox, and as discerning and prophetically perceptive as an eagle. (See Ezekiel 1:5–10.)

Again, in my vision, the wheels were moving; wherever they went, the glory was displayed with great power. These wheels moved over various regions and territories, carrying the impact of the glory. When the lightning would flash from the outer rim of the wheels, it would ignite another hub, which then grew spokes and formed an outer rim: wheels creating wheels!

I believe that God is moving upon His people to establish creative hubs on the earth. These are hubs where creatives gather and nurture one another as they worship the Lord through various forms of creativity, each one contributing their specific talents and giftings. This connectedness will provide a space for the purposes of God to develop and flow out to the world, releasing the greater glory. And the power manifested will also release an impartation of creativity to others.

UNIFYING GLORY AND CREATIVE GLORY

Unity in the Spirit among believers is essential for these creative-glory hubs to exist and make an impact for the kingdom. Just before His death and resurrection, Jesus prayed to the Father,

I have given them the glory that you gave me, that they may be one as we are one—I in them and you in me—so that they may be brought to complete unity. Then the world will know that you sent me and have loved them even as you have loved me. (John 17:22–23 NIV)

This is an extremely important word from the Lord to us. Jesus was praying for all believers, and He said that He wanted us to be one with each other, just as He is one with the Father. To accomplish this, Jesus has given us the glory of the Father. Unity in the body of Christ can be achieved only in the glory that He gives us. Therefore, what we need today is *unifying glory that produces creative glory*. And I believe that creative glory will also lead us to cultivate unifying glory. It works both ways.

I love connecting with other ministries that move in the power of the Spirit. In that connection, there is a convergence of anointings. Creative glory comes to bring us together and join our individual giftings with the greater purposes of God.

All of our creative endeavors are ultimately accomplished in the context of community—beginning with the community of our relationship with the Father, Son, and Spirit. Through the Son, in the name of the Father, the Holy Spirit brings heavenly ideas and innovations to us. The Spirit works within us, flowing creative works through us—often in conjunction with other people—to those who will benefit from them.

We may sometimes work alone in our creativity, but that is only one part of the process. For example, artists often need other people to assist them in bringing their works to the attention of the public. Scriptwriters need producers, directors, actors, and others to bring their stories to life. Whatever endeavors we engage in, we need other people, in some capacity, to make those endeavors successful and be the best they can be. If there's anything I've learned about the creative process, it is this: creativity sparks creativity!

A DIVINE JOINING

Remember that creative glory naturally progresses from unifying glory. The late Ruth Ward Heflin wrote about this important theme in her book *Unifying Glory*. She asks:

What is unifying glory?

- ✦ It is the touch of glory that brings a divine joining of brother to brother.

- ✦ It is the miraculous uniting of the diverse members of the family of God.

- ✦ It is the answer to the prayer of Jesus: "That they all may be one."[37]

Unifying Glory was one of the last books Sister Ruth wrote before she stepped over into her eternal reward more than two decades ago. She was a forerunner in the glory, and I honor her because so much of the ministry that Janet and I are doing today was imparted to us through her faith and teachings. As I mentioned in the preface to this book, I didn't know Sister Ruth personally, and I never had the privilege of attending any of her meetings. She never laid her hands directly on me in prayer. Nevertheless, she left an indelible deposit of her anointing upon me through the books that she wrote.

As a teenager, when I initially came into an understanding of the spiritual realities of the glory realm, God taught me about singing in the Spirit, singing the new song, and moving in the glory. Sister Ruth's first book, *Glory: Experiencing the Atmosphere of Heaven*, greatly helped me to understand what God was teaching me. I also read her books *Revival Glory* and *River Glory*. Then, in my twenties, I read the rest of her "glory" books: *Golden Glory*, *Harvest Glory*, *Unifying Glory*, and *Revelation Glory*.

God used these books and other sources to help me connect the spiritual dots. Ruth's books are still available today, and I encourage you to read all of them. Such a tremendous impartation came to me from each of them that I can never doubt the power of spiritual conveyance. This refers to the anointing on someone's life being transferred to others not only through direct contact but also through that person's works: writings, musical recordings, artwork, and so on. As I expressed earlier, the impartation that those books gave me inspired me to write my own books on the glory realm and to believe that people worldwide would receive an impartation from them as well.

---

37. Ruth Ward Heflin, *Unifying Glory* (Hagerstown, MD: McDougal Publishing, 2000), back cover.

> CREATIVE GLORY COMES TO BRING US TOGETHER
> AND JOIN OUR INDIVIDUAL GIFTINGS WITH
> THE GREATER PURPOSES OF GOD.

UNITY IN DIVERSITY

Unifying glory is a powerful spiritual reality. I love the passage from John 17 that we read earlier in this chapter. I love the truth that Jesus was and is one with the Father and that He wants us to be one with the Father, too, as well as with other believers: *"That they may be one as we are one...so that they may be brought to complete unity"* (John 17:22–23). Jesus felt that this oneness was very important, so we should too. Unity among believers affects our ability to successfully share the gospel so that others can come to the saving knowledge of Christ.

Jesus continued, *"Then* [when we have finally achieved the unity He desires] *the world will know that you sent me and have loved them even as you have loved me"* (verse 23). Until that happens, the world will not know this truth.

The reality is that, as children of God, we are one in Christ. Unity is not just some grandiose or fantastical idea. Jesus prayed for it, so the concept was born in the very heart of God, and it must be possible.

As Ruth Heflin said, unifying glory is "the touch of glory that brings a divine joining of brother to brother. It is a miraculous uniting of the diverse members of the family of God. It is the answer to the prayer of Jesus: 'That they all may be one.'"[38] Today, we don't give nearly enough emphasis to this vital truth.

Somehow, we in the body of Christ must become examples to the hurting world around us. More than ever before, the world needs us to rise and shine, to be unified, to exemplify oneness. How can we expect the world to be healed if the church itself cannot first be healed? How can we expect the world to be united when the church is so divided? The church must lead by example, and only Jesus can unite us.

---

38. Heflin, back cover.

Jesus said, *"Blessed are the peacemakers, for they will be called children of God"* (Matthew 5:9 NIV). Christians are often divided about issues and doctrines and traditions, but God loves those who promote peace among His people. Instead of focusing on what divides us, let's focus on what unites us, and let's ask the Holy Spirit to teach us what we need to do in this regard.

Over and over again, we hear believers declaring their stand on this issue and that issue. They are adamant to make their point, and they believe theirs is the only right way to think or believe. This approach is clearly detrimental to the overall welfare of the body of Christ. The first step we need to take is to emphasize the positives of Christianity—starting and ending with Jesus! If we focus on Jesus and the desire of His heart for us to be united, we can make a huge difference worldwide. God is one, so we must be one. Period!

Unfortunately, there can be so much competition within the church—often within worship teams and among creative people. This issue isn't a modern problem; it's actually an age-old dilemma that started in heaven. At one point, Lucifer, one of God's archangels, became proud and exalted in his own sight, somehow believing that he could become even more beautiful than God Himself. (See Isaiah 14:12–14.) As a result, he fell from his pure angelic state and rebelled against God while encouraging other angels to rebel against Him too. (See Revelation 12:3–4.) When we look at ourselves and our human ability more than we look to God and His divine ability, it is a slippery slope toward self-glorification. This is a demonic doorway that opens the way to every trouble.

AS CHILDREN OF GOD, WE ARE ONE IN CHRIST!

"WHAT FLAVOR ARE YOU?"

Once, when I met another believer for the first time, they quickly asked me, "What flavor of Christian are you?" I understand their asking that question. There are undeniable denominational and theological differences among Christians, and they wanted to know where I stood on certain issues.

However, surely, if Jesus envisioned unity, we can too. And, if we can envision it, then we can all work toward it.

To give a simple example, there are certain flavors of food that are more pleasing to me than others. In our family of five, each of us has a variety of tastes that we enjoy more than others. That doesn't mean we don't all love each other and that we can't agree on the larger, more important issues of life. Who is to say that one flavor is better than another? For example, I like ham and pineapple on my pizza; Janet likes a "triple crown" of pepperoni, green peppers, and mushrooms; and each of our children have their own preferences. But we all enjoy pizza!

Likewise, even though there are a variety of "toppings," or denominations, all Christians have the same love for Jesus. The startling reality is that there are currently more than 200 Christian denominations in the United States and more than 45,000 Christian denominations worldwide![39] Those numbers don't even include all the nondenominational churches. But, with Jesus, the King of kings and Lord of lords, as our Common Denominator, unity is possible. After all, what seems impossible for humans is possible with God. (See, for example, Mark 10:27.)

Together we are better. Together we are blessed. This is the fruit of creative glory!

UNITED FOR EMPOWERMENT

What we focus on we empower. When we focus on divisions, we strengthen those divisions, creating more walls. We should be doing our best to tear down walls, not create new ones. God teaches us in His Word and by His Spirit that what we speak has the power of life and death. (See Proverbs 18:21.) Our words and actions have the ability to create realities and change atmospheres. Therefore, we must be promotors of unity.

We must live in unity, and we must proclaim unity. To do that, we must stop declaring to anyone who will listen that our way is the only way when it comes to lesser or nonessential issues. Let God deal with those issues. As Christians, let's make a prayerful, serious choice to declare and promote what does unite us—Jesus and building the kingdom of God on earth.

39. Donavyn Coffey, "Why Does Christianity Have So Many Denominations?" *LiveScience*, February 27, 2021, https://www.livescience.com/christianity-denominations.html.

Although God's people are physically scattered worldwide, we must come together in mind and spirit to make the most significant impact for the advancement of His kingdom. God is doing His part to facilitate this union, but we must do our part as well. A united church is a powerful church.

CONNECTING WORLDWIDE

Throughout history, God has brought His people together in very unusual and powerful ways. It is no different today. During the coronavirus pandemic, many believers found themselves isolated at home, unable to go to their workplaces or travel very far. In many areas, church services either were not allowed or were limited, so Christians weren't congregating in person as they love to do and as is directed in the Bible. (See, for example, Ezra 3:1; Nehemiah 8:1; Matthew 18:20, Acts 14:27; Hebrews 10:25.) But even with the government-mandated prohibitions on groups of people assembling in churches and other private and public places, God opened other avenues for believers to "gather." One of those avenues was to connect online for church services, Bible studies, and prayer meetings, often through social media platforms and podcasts. Millions of Christians have communicated with each other through these venues. Many have shared testimonies and built healthy relationships with other believers that they otherwise would never have met. The Lord provided these creative ways for His people to stay in touch with Him and each other locally, nationally, and globally.

This is exactly what happened to me when, during the lockdown, I was challenged to find a way to continue to reach out to God's people. For twenty years, I had been traveling across the United States and around the world to minister. Suddenly, travel was restricted, and, for months at a time, I could no longer do that. One day, during those first few challenging weeks, Janet and I realized that the U.S. National Day of Prayer would be held on the following Sunday. We felt in our hearts that we should reach out through social media to those who followed our ministry, offering our prayer support and encouragement during that difficult time.

We didn't have the media savvy or technical know-how to put together a sophisticated-looking program. However, we did know how to turn on our phones and tablets and livestream through an online platform. So, that's what we did. The response was phenomenal! We felt so blessed to be able to encourage and minister to others in this new way, and the feedback we received let us know that others were being blessed as well. We decided to do it again, this time on a Tuesday night.

Something that we've learned in moving with the Spirit is that if God is blessing what you're doing, then do it more. The touch of God's glory came upon our Tuesday-night meetings, so we continued to meet in this way week after week, streaming through Facebook and YouTube. We eventually called this ministry time *Glory Bible Study*. Through these weekly online gatherings, a glory community of like-minded believers began to form. Neither Janet nor I can take the credit for what God did to bring together this awesome community of people from all over the world. It was His idea before we even had a clue what He was leading us to do. We simply followed His direction and were led by the wind of His Spirit.

During this time, I also had the privilege of ministering online with one of our dear friends, Pastor Georg Karl, of Stuttgart, Germany. When I talked with him early in the pandemic, I asked, "How are things going with your ministry there?" I was surprised by his answer:

> It is absolutely amazing what God is doing at Glory Life Center here in Stuttgart! Although we are not able to have church in the auditorium, I "stream" live miracle services. During the services, we encourage people who are watching to call in, and our church members operate the phones from wherever they are. Many people calling in have never stepped into a church, but God is bringing them in now through the Internet. Many of the callers have never attended a Pentecostal church or a charismatic meeting or otherwise participated with this flavor of Christianity. Yet they are excited and receiving a touch from God, and they're being brought together.

Yes, God's unifying glory is at work on earth right now. You might look around and say, "I still see this problem and that problem in the church; I still see this division and that division." Yes, but look around again, this time lifting your eyes higher. Look toward heaven, toward Jesus, and join His prayer for unity in the body.

COMPLEMENTING AND SUPPORTING EACH OTHER

In the book of 1 Chronicles, we read how David encouraged his son Solomon regarding the building of the temple:

> *You have a large number of skilled stonemasons and carpenters and craftsmen of every kind. You have expert goldsmiths and silversmiths and workers of bronze and iron. Now begin the work, and may the LORD be with you!* (1 Chronicles 22:15–16 NLT)

The ancient Israelites were about to construct a temple for God, and an abundance of workmen had been called upon to help build it. What does this have to do with us in the twenty-first century? A lot! First, in the realms of God, among the people of God (including you and me), there is an abundance of workers with talents, abilities, and giftings—an abundance of creativity. That creativity does not come to us solely in the natural. Trades can be learned, and we can develop our natural skills and grow in those areas. But we must understand that, as believers, everything good that flows through our lives comes from the Holy Spirit. God wants to give you heavenly skills, heavenly talents, heavenly abilities that will cause you to arise and work successfully at whatever you do, knowing that the Lord is working with you.

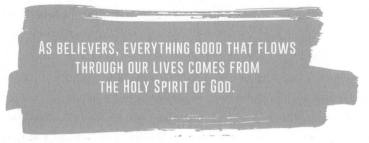

AS BELIEVERS, EVERYTHING GOOD THAT FLOWS THROUGH OUR LIVES COMES FROM THE HOLY SPIRIT OF GOD.

A CHURCH FILLED WITH CREATIVE GLORY

It is amazing to think about the various workers who helped to construct the temple. Those who worked on this special project are described as *"willing"* (1 Chronicles 28:21). And the leaders of the Israelites gave generously toward the building of the temple. (See 1 Chronicles 29:1–20.) This is how I picture the temple workers working together as they employed their skills: They were not competing with one another. They were not trying to see who was best or who could garner the most attention. Each one knew what they were asked to do, and they did it as unto the Lord. Each one had a specific call, a specific assignment, and each one answered their call and completed their assignment to the best of their ability, the Lord working with them. The result was that the work was accomplished, it was done well, and it was completed in good time.

We must not waste our energies criticizing others. It saddens my heart when I see this happen in the church. When those who don't know the Lord criticize or complain, that may be understandable. However, when I see believers—even ministers—doing it, I have to wonder what motivates them. What good is an opportunity that comes at the expense of demeaning others? Seeking to exalt one's ministry over the ministries of others is not a righteous pursuit. This is not a time for competition. We need to recognize the truth of this statement: *"Every kingdom divided against itself is brought to desolation; and every city or house divided against itself shall not stand"* (Matthew 12:25 KJVER). Instead of causing or perpetuating division, we must reach out and join hands with other believers, unifying the people of God. The body of Christ must come together in the Spirit. Then God will have His way in and through us.

Creative glory unifies God's people in supernatural ways. It blesses my heart when I see or hear about various ministries joining hands, especially in these challenging times. They are saying to each other, "I want to help you. I want to elevate you. I want us to work together for kingdom purposes in our city, our region, and our nation."

I was recently given a postcard-sized print of a beautiful painting called *The Great Return* by Barbara Louise Buchli. In this painting, the Lord of glory is clothed as the King of kings, wearing a royal crown and a stately robe. He is riding on the back of a white horse, surrounded by hosts of angels, and He is descending from the clouds for His earthly return.

Barbara created this artwork after having a prophetic vision in which Jesus appeared to her and spoke these words: "Paint Me in all My glory. I'm returning soon. My people are still looking at Me on the cross. You've seen Me. Paint Me as I truly am. I am returning soon, and My people are not ready."

The Spirit brought an urgent message for Barbara to paint the *now* reality of Jesus. It's true that many people still think of Christ in the crucifix position, hanging in agony, worn and beaten, His body defeated by the enemy spirit. But we must lift our eyes to the heavens in order to see the greatest part of the story! Jesus has risen in triumph over sin and the grave. Creative glory opens our eyes to see what is happening right now in the spiritual dimensions. In this way, we are given the privilege of sharing and spreading God's *now* message through the arts and other creative avenues. We should expect creative glory to bring greater visions to God's people in these days.

The emphasis of Jesus's prophetic message is "I am returning soon." But when Jesus returns, He's not coming back for a people divided by petty issues or living with intolerance toward one another. He is returning for a beautiful and gracious church, a church filled with creative glory. When we come together, there is so much more beauty. We need every part of the body joined together in its rightful place.

Creative glory enables believers to flow as one in heavenly unity. During turbulent times, when it seems like everything is falling apart around us, God desires for His body to come together as a sign and a wonder of His goodness, His power, and the salvation that only Jesus can offer.

The Lord is divinely connecting the dots for us, removing obstacles and bringing together what only He can. He is eliminating distractions, divisions, and ungodly attitudes, and He is creating a glorious church. He is bringing us together in creative glory in much the same way that He brought together the dry bones Ezekiel saw in that infamous valley we read about in Ezekiel 37:1–14. Reviewing those dry bones, the Spirit challenged Ezekiel, *"Can these bones live?"* (verse 3 ESV, AMP, KJVER, NIV). Then the Spirit spoke, and there was a sudden rattling of the bones. Not only did the Spirit cause these bones to come together, but He also attached tendons and flesh to them. Then He began to breathe life into them. What had been dry, sun-bleached bones became vibrant bodies, an army for God.

Today, God's creative glory is bringing all the pieces together for the body of Christ to rise up and be seen as the beautiful bride it was meant to be. Jesus is coming back for a bride without spot or wrinkle. (See Ephesians 5:27.) And that's something only God can do.

CREATIVE GLORY! LET THIS GLORY ARISE IN ME!

CREATIVE RELEASE

"I knew you before I formed you in your mother's womb.
Before you were born I set you apart and appointed you as my
prophet to the nations."
—Jeremiah 1:5 (NLT)

God wants to release His creative glory in your life!

Are you ready to receive it? Or are you still wondering how God could use you due to your past mistakes, failures, and disappointments?

I have found that many people hold back from receiving all that God has for them because they feel unworthy to receive it. You may have experienced many difficulties and setbacks in life, but God wants to infuse you with His glory.

RELEASE FEELINGS OF UNWORTHINESS

Long before you were born, God formed you, carefully knitting together every part of your being—spirit, soul, and body. He made you for a unique purpose: to carry a special anointing into every place He leads you on the journey of life. Much of the resistance you've experienced, the hardships you've endured, and the pain you've walked through was an enemy assignment designed to stop the call of God on your life. But, by God's grace, you're still here! Your life is a living testimony of His faithfulness through the good and the bad.

You've weathered some storms and risen above the torrents that attempted to dismantle your peace. Now you're being called to take the very things that the enemy meant for harm and use them as a weapon of light against the darkness. God has given you creative glory to help you overcome the greatest challenges of life. When you learn to release your pain to the Spirit as an offering, it becomes a powerful spiritual tool.

RELEASE "ORDINARINESS"

Other people may not feel unworthy, but they don't think they were meant to do anything extraordinary in life. If that has been your perspective, it will take a lot of courage for you to step out of the ordinary mindset you've been taught to live in and step into your creative self, the YOU that God created to exist. However, the anointing of the Spirit comes with the courage you need to take that step, so receive it right now. Lift your hands to the Lord and praise Him for freeing you from false thinking and the grip of fear. Sense the life-giving freedom of the Spirit enabling you to be YOU-nique.

+ Thank God that, through Jesus, He's removed all shame and guilt as well as the bondage of sin from your life.

+ Thank God that, through Jesus, He's given you a fresh beginning and enough faith to get started.

+ Thank God that He created you in His image and that you reflect His glory on the earth.

GOD HAS GIVEN YOU CREATIVE GLORY TO HELP YOU OVERCOME THE GREATEST CHALLENGES OF LIFE.

A GIFT THAT KEEPS ON GIVING

Many people who grew up in the 1960s, 70s, and 80s will remember the names of brothers Sid and Marty Krofft. Their children's shows, such as *H.R. Pufnstuf*, *The Bugaloos*, *Lidsville*, and *Land of the Lost*, were Saturday-morning staples. Sid is the equivalent of Walt Disney for those generations. Creating vibrantly colored and zany television shows, his imagination clearly operated in an out-of-this-world way.

I recently had the chance to speak with Sid Krofft, who is an artistic and creative genius. Born in Montreal, Canada, but raised in Providence, Rhode Island, Sid came from a family of very simple means. He told me the following:

> I was totally self-taught. I did not come from a theatrical family, and they had no clue about show business. I just built my own little empire. I knew nothing about puppets.

> Puppeteers, in those days, were like magicians. It was handed down from generation to generation. They had their own tricks that were secretive, you know, how they strung their puppets and how their puppets did all these incredible things. I had no clue. I created everything all by myself. But I'm sure that we are born with that kind of a gift.

From that gift, Sid began his career as a puppeteer in vaudeville. He later toured with the Ringling Bros. and Barnum & Bailey Circus. Eventually, he was "discovered" by Judy Garland, and he became the opening act for her first world tour. Over the years, Sid has had a number of opportunities and has experienced many divine connections, traveling with such notables as Liberace, Frank Sinatra, the Andrew Sisters, and others. Most of all, however, his life has been filled with creativity.

I asked Sid if he'd ever met Walt Disney, and he told me this story:

> I toured with Tony Martin and Cyd Charisse, and we were having lunch at the Polo Lounge in the Beverly Hills Hotel. Walt Disney was sitting at the next table, and I was literally just shaking. We had never met him before. I had written him a letter when I was ten years old, and he had answered me. I asked him if I could do a puppet show of Pinocchio in my backyard because it was 1940 and the music had

just come out. He said, "Yes, but you can't charge any money, and I'll be watching over you."

Anyhow, as we were sitting at the restaurant, Walt Disney came over to say hello, and I was literally shaking. We were introduced to him. My brother Marty was with me, and when Walt walked over, he said, "Oh yeah, I've heard of you guys. But I'd like to give you some advice. Always put your name above everything that you create because someday it's gonna be worth something." And he was right!

When creative people get together, creative things happen!

The day after his ninety-second birthday, I asked Sid what inspired him on a day-to-day basis. He said, "Life...waking up! Every day is my birthday. Enjoy life! Don't wait for a number to give somebody a gift or to congratulate them, because every day is a gift that must be celebrated."

This kind of attitude will keep you in the ebb and flow of creativity. We must learn to see life as a gift that keeps giving. It is in this posture that great ideas come. I also asked Sid where he received the inspiration for creating some of his television series, and he told me the following:

I'm a runner. But now I walk a couple of miles, and the adrenaline kicks in. When it kicks in, as a runner, that's where I created most of my shows—down at the beach. I would run nine miles, and, after the second mile, oh wow, you can create the world. You know, that's where *Lidsville* came from...on the beach.... The wind took my hat, and I thought, "Wow! Wait a minute! There's a show here. Why am I running after a hat? Screaming at a hat?" I said, "Come back," and the wind just took my favorite hat, so it became a show.

Sid also told me that brilliant ideas sometimes come to him from his nighttime dreams. "I dream every night. My mind's going all the time. I have a pad of paper next to my bed."

We have to learn to capture ideas as they come. As quickly as they appear, they can also disappear if we don't write them down fast enough or flow in that direction. Creative glory helps us to stay in the flow.

At the end of our conversation, Sid said, "We all have creativity. Everybody has been given that. It's just that some people don't use it."

CREATIVE GLORY BRINGS PERSONAL GROWTH

Are you ready to use the creativity God has given you? Are you ready to join with those whom God has provided to work with you or help you along the way?

Don't hold back! Let go of any reservations or preconceived ideas you may have that you lack creativity or are unworthy to be used by God. As has famously been said, "Let go and let God do what *He* wants to do."

I was designed by God to create, and so were you. There is no one else like you in all the world. Not only that, but there has *never been* anyone else like you in all of history, and there never will be. In creative glory, we are free to do everything we've been created to do. Remember, God made you, and, through the finished work of Christ, you have been forgiven of all your sins. God accepts you, and He is ready to reveal Himself in new ways to the world through you.

Your creativity is important to God, to you, and to others; it can be life-changing when you choose to share it. Not only can it change other people who embrace it, but it can change you, as well, from the inside out. We experience personal growth as we let go of the past—and creativity allows us the freedom to do this in a healthy way.

In many ways, creative expression allows us to move "*from glory to glory*" (2 Corinthians 3:18 KJVER, NKJV). It helps to remove the spiritual, mental, and physical blockages that have hindered us. Writing a song about your encounters with God or other people, painting a picture out of the depth of your experiences, dancing in sync with your feelings—all of these expressions will help to release you and move you forward. There is no need to hold back, because you were created to create. When you keep an upward focus, your life becomes a beautiful fragrance of worship to the Lord. This, in turn, releases the beauty of His glory back to the earth.

> IN CREATIVE GLORY, WE ARE FREE TO DO EVERYTHING WE'VE BEEN CREATED TO DO.

ORDINARY PEOPLE DOING EXTRAORDINARY THINGS

When "ordinary" people invite the Spirit into the creative process, they can do extraordinary things. Remember, creative glory brings the *extra* to our *ordinary*. It places the *super* over our *natural*. In this way, our creativity becomes a supernatural display of heavenly glory. The evangelist Winkie Pratney said, "Those that God used in the past were just ordinary people with an extraordinary Master."[40] And that's the truth! We see this confirmed throughout the Scriptures in the lives of God's people. Take, for example, the following flawed heroes of our faith:

+ Abraham and his wife, Sarah, were beyond the natural age for having a child. Yet, because Abraham believed God's promise that he would have a son, he became the father of many nations. (See, for example, Genesis 17:3–7.)

+ Joseph was abused by his brothers, but he didn't allow his pain to define him. Instead of being a victim, he chose to become victorious. This led to his living in a palace and saving his extended family—which included the direct line of the Messiah—from starvation. (See Genesis 37; 39:1–47:11.)

+ Rahab was a prostitute living in a city that was about to be decimated in battle. But, by faith, she chose to align herself with the Lord and His people, and she and her family were spared from destruction. (See Joshua 2; 6:17, 25; Hebrews 11:31; James 2:25.)

+ David was an adulterer and a murderer, but the Lord restored his life after he returned to Him with a deeply repentant heart. (See 2 Samuel 11:1–12:25; Psalm 51.)

+ Moses had a speech impediment and had murdered an Egyptian, but when he yielded his life to the Lord, God used him to lead the Hebrew people out of slavery and on the road to the promised land. (See, for example, Exodus 4:10–17; 14:1–15:20.)

+ Gideon was the least in his family and came from the least of the tribes of Israel. He was fearful and was totally unqualified to lead an army. But because he was obedient to God, he experienced great victory, defeating 135,000 experienced soldiers! (See Judges 6–8:21.)

---

40. Winkey Pratney, "Winkey Pratney Quotes," Quote Fancy, https://quotefancy.com/winkie-pratney-quotes.

- Mary Magdalene was demon-possessed, but she was delivered by Jesus and became one of His most devoted followers. And she was given the privilege of being the first to see Him after His resurrection. (See Mark 16:9–10.)

- Paul (originally named Saul) vehemently persecuted believers of the early church. However, after he encountered the resurrected Jesus on the road to Damascus and surrendered His life to the Lord, he became a dedicated apostle of Jesus. Paul passionately served the Lord for the rest of his life, building the church and writing nearly half the books of the New Testament (amounting to about a third of its contents). (See Acts 9:1–19; 22:3–17; 26:12–18; 1 Corinthians 15:9.)

- John Mark was an immature believer who abandoned Paul and Barnabas during a missionary journey. Through the spiritual encouragement of Barnabas, John Mark grew in the Lord and was later reconciled with Paul and served with him in the proclamation of the gospel. (See Acts 13:4–14; 15:36–41; 2 Timothy 4:10–11.)

Creative glory has always helped God's chosen people to turn setbacks into setups to fulfill His divine purposes. Each one of these men and women had their own natural inadequacies and reasons why they might be disqualified from doing something great for God. Yet their names are recorded within the sacred pages of the Bible, and their stories have been told from generation to generation. We celebrate these believers who learned to overcome their challenges and pain by submitting their lives to God by faith.

In the same way, despite our weaknesses, creative glory comes to teach us, lift us, and propel us beyond the difficulties we've faced. It helps us to turn bad situations around and enables us to come forth from the fire as pure gold. (See Job 23:10.)

As believers, our primary assignment is to carry an atmosphere of God's glory and radiate His light wherever we go. Everybody wants to stay close to people who feel like warm sunshine. The world needs to know about God's love—and to really *feel* it. Your creative anointing will be the light that shines on the darkest of days, bringing warmth, comfort, and clarity of vision. Your creative gifts can also be like a beautiful rainbow that appears in the middle of a rainstorm, bringing the promise of hope to those who need it the most.

Creative glory is given to us not so that attention will be drawn toward us (the creation) but so that attention will be drawn toward God (the Creator). What we create for His glory brings Him glory. If we keep this perspective in mind, it will free us from any feelings of competition or comparison with others. What we do, we do for God alone.

LEARN HOW TO MOVE WITH CREATIVE GLORY

When I was sixteen, I had a life-changing encounter with the Spirit. I had been raised in the church, and, until that time, I knew a lot about God and Jesus but very little about the Holy Spirit. Yet, after that initial encounter, the Spirit taught and trained me in praise and worship. He gave me songs to sing. I would sit at the piano, and the Spirit would show me what keys to play and how to play them. This is how I learned to play the piano: by the direction, counsel, and instruction of the Holy Spirit. And I learned at warp speed—my training was supernaturally accelerated.

I had not necessarily been interested in learning to play the piano, but that was what God was doing in my heart. In today's vocabulary, I received a heavenly "download." Within three years, I had written about six hundred songs. Some of them were published, but most were not; they were given to me by the Spirit as a personal gift. That impartation of creative glory changed my life.

When we create anything, it's important to move *with* the flow of creative glory and *not* against it. Solomon delivered this important advice in Psalm 127:1: *"Unless the Lord builds a house, the work of the builders is wasted"* (NLT). In this regard, we might want to consider our desire to work on any creative endeavor in the same way a responsible worker would approach their part in the building of a house: we must all submit to the Master Builder.

Jesus confirmed this truth when He spoke to Peter about how the church would succeed and grow: *"I will build my church, and all the powers of hell will not conquer it"* (Matthew 16:18 NLT). When creative glory becomes our guiding source of inspiration, no opposing force can prevent the development and completion of what God wants to do through us.

In the early years of my ministry, when I had additional jobs on the side to support my calling, I worked at a members-only big-box store. I didn't have a fancy job at the store, like being a cashier or a door greeter, or a position working in the corporate offices. I worked in what they called the box bin. Do you know what that is? I didn't…until I was hired for the job. The box bin was a room surrounded by chain-link fencing and filled with all the empty cardboard boxes from the warehouse. My job was to cut down every box and make it suitable to be reused by those who needed a way to carry home their purchases.

I was in that box bin all day long by myself, and being in there made me feel like I was in prison. But even in the middle of the box bin, my heart would begin to swirl with creative glory, and the Spirit would bring me new songs to sing. I knew that if I didn't capture the inspiration of a song immediately, I wouldn't remember it. So, right there in the box bin, I would tear off a piece of cardboard and write down the lyrics as they came to me. It only took a few seconds to write down those lyrics. When I was finished writing, I would stick that piece of cardboard in my pocket so that the lyrics were ready for me to work on further when I got back home. In this way, I learned how to move with the flow of creative glory in my particular circumstances.

I eventually recorded one of those box-bin songs on my first worship album, *Waterfall*. The song is called "I Surrender My Heart," and I sang it as a duet with my mom. Many of my early worship songs were written in a similar way. I'm so glad that I've learned how to flow with creative glory, and it's my prayer that you'll begin to flow with it too!

WHEN WE CREATE ANYTHING, IT'S IMPORTANT TO MOVE WITH THE FLOW OF CREATIVE GLORY AND NOT AGAINST IT.

ACCESSING CREATIVE GLORY

How can we more completely access God's creative glory? Here are five practical ways.

FIVE PRACTICAL WAYS TO CONNECT WITH CREATIVE GLORY

BE ESTABLISHED IN GOD'S LOVE

To be fully creative, you must know that you are loved! Once you recognize that you are truly loved and valued by your Creator, your creative gifts will begin to flourish. Then, as you build loving, supportive human relationships with other believers, you can express even more fully the creativity God has given you.

When I was much younger, I used to really enjoy drawing, and I always did my best creative works within the context of loving relationships. If I wrote letters to my friends, I would spend hours doodling and coloring all over them, even decorating the envelopes with drawings of cartoon characters and anything else that my young imagination could think of. (To this day, when I meet some of my old friends from those days, they tell me that they've held on to my letters all these years because of the artwork that covers them!)

Kids do this all the time—they create drawings and artwork for their beloved moms and dads, brothers and sisters, grandmas and grandpas, or special friends. When you were growing up, you might not have had a loving family, and so you may not have expressed yourself artistically in this way. You may not have a supportive family today who will nurture your creativity. This doesn't need to hinder your creativity. I like the following saying: "Friends are the family we choose." And that is so true! Regardless of your past relationships, within the body of Christ, you are welcomed and loved because God created you, He calls you His child, and He has placed you within His family.

One impediment to experiencing the freedom to create is fear. This is one of the biggest obstacles every creator needs to overcome. Here again, we must overcome fear through love because, as the Bible says, *"There is no fear in love; but perfect love casts out fear"* (1 John 4:18 NKJV). Fear can grip our lives for a number of reasons: maybe you've been rejected by others, maybe your talents have been misunderstood, or maybe you just don't "fit in" to the general mold of society and this has caused you to feel anxious and intimidated about expressing yourself creatively. Whatever it may be, you must realize that fear paralyzes dreams, whereas the love of God liberates them. In a loving atmosphere, you can grow, thrive, and succeed.

I encourage you to seek out friends, associates, and a church community where people share a special appreciation for diverse expressions of creativity and where you will feel welcomed and loved. It may take a little while to find like-minded people, but don't give up!

Again, I've been able to be very creative when I've felt loved. I think everybody does! On the other hand, I feel my creative flow being blocked when I'm fearful about something. Fear inhibits, but love releases. It's important to recognize your fears and face them head-on. Don't suppress them—doing so will only empower them and keep your creativity bound. Ask for God's help and look for the assistance He sends you; it may come from His creative angels. Remember, fear shuts you down, but love wakes you up! God is a champion of creativity. He celebrates you and all the gifts He has given you.

ALLOW CREATIVITY TO SPARK CREATIVITY

The flame from one candle can light the wick of another candle. This is the way it works in the natural world, but this is also a spiritual and emotional principle. Your creativity can be ignited—or squelched—by your daily influences. Take time each day to be inspired by other creative people and their work. For example, you could read the biography of an inspirational leader. When I was young and interested in animation, I read many books about Shamus Culhane, Walt Disney, Walter Lantz, and Chuck Jones, among others. These books inspired me to create my own cartoon characters and work on other imaginative projects. Later, when the Spirit was moving me into full-time ministry, I began reading books about many of the great revivalists of the past, like Smith Wigglesworth, John G. Lake, Maria Woodworth-Etter, A. A. Allen, Aimee Semple McPherson, and others. Their stories helped me to learn from the mistakes they made and inspired me to continue walking in the victories they achieved.

Another way you might spark creativity is to go to a local art museum and take time to really appreciate the artwork—looking at it from different perspectives and allowing your imagination to be expanded. You might consider attending a theater show or symphony orchestra concert in town. Visit a place you've never visited before in your city. Eat at a new restaurant or try your hand at making a new recipe; experiment with flavors and unusual food combinations. There is a man at our church who loves baking. He bakes with excellence, and, on several occasions, he has baked our family cookies and cakes that carry a revelatory prophetic message! One time, he made us an "Angel Food Cake" covered with golden sprinkles and placed it on a golden plate. While he was preparing it, he prayed for our family and ministry. This was very meaningful to us and a creative way to bless our family. He told me that he likes to invite the Spirit to guide him in the process of choosing ingredients and in specific ways of preparing his baked goods. His time in the glory inspires his time in the kitchen!

One final idea is to try doing something you've never done before by watching an online tutorial video and following the instructions. These are all practical ways to get the fire started, so to speak. You should try something new at least once a week. If you've been in a creative rut, doing this should move you into action!

CONNECT WITH THE CREATOR'S HANDIWORK

Enjoy God's creation and allow it to energize you. It's important to take time to literally "smell the roses." I'm not sure who exactly came up with that saying, but it's amazing how refreshed and energized you'll feel after taking a short break to enjoy nature. Whether it is a stroll through a garden or field, a walk through a forest, or a trip to a coastline to see the ocean, being in the midst of God's creation has the ability to ignite a fresh spark of creative glory in your life.

Recently, I took my two daughters, Liberty and Legacy, on a short daddy-daughter trip. We went to the Florida panhandle for a relaxing getaway. While we walked together on the powdery white beach, we began to notice the windswept designs—beautiful formations that appeared across the sand. I even commented to the girls, "Wow, I would love that pattern as a wallpaper print in the living room!" It was God's creative signature seen in the sand.

Legacy noticed the many different shells spread around the beach. She reached down to pick one up, showed me its unique brown-and-white design, and said, "Look, God made this one too!" I reminded her that each and every shell is different, specially designed by God. We began to see His handiwork everywhere we looked. There's just something about spending time in nature that brings refreshment and energy to the soul.

SURROUND YOURSELF WITH A CREATIVE ATMOSPHERE

In addition to surrounding yourself with nature, surround yourself with other creative atmospheres. Everyone is wired differently, so something that inspires me may not necessarily inspire you. Find the things that stir up your individual creativity. Begin to take notice of the music, colors, and fragrances that help you to deeply sense God's glory. For instance, there is music that we like, and then there is music that makes every nerve in our body come alive and feel the very presence of God! Learn to create an atmosphere that is conducive to becoming spiritually alive. This may include hanging on the wall some of your favorite Scripture verses or placing on your desk a work of art that reminds you of God's constant companionship. Our home is filled with prophetic artwork, biblically themed statues, anointed music, and framed Scripture verses that are very meaningful to us. All these things help to inspire us and set the proper mood so that we can be productive in creative glory.

FIND THE TOOLS YOU NEED

Finding the tools you need might mean purchasing a computer program, a phone app, art supplies, a musical instrument, office equipment, or something as simple as a notebook. There is nothing worse than being inspired to do something but feeling like you don't have the proper tools to work with in order to express your creativity. Only you know what you need. You may not have the money to purchase an expensive tool or instrument, so start where you are and work with what you already have. Learn how to improvise the tools you need, and have them ready for when you need them. Then, as you progress along the road of your creative journey by building your faith, using your gifts, and saving your money, you can invest in the more expensive items to help you in your creative call.

I always like to have a reliable pen and thick pad of paper near my bedside because, at times, I awaken in the middle of the night with a great book idea, and I always want to be sure to write it down and capture it in the moment it comes to me. As I mentioned previously, I've learned that inspiration can go away just as quickly as it comes if we're not ready to catch it! I leave a keyboard set up in my home so that when a new song starts flowing, I can easily sit down and find the chord structure for it and record it onto my phone. I also have a drawer in my tool bench that's filled with art supplies—paints, brushes, pencils, sponges—all ready for quick retrieval when inspiration strikes! Having the proper tools easily accessible helps you to capture the flow of creative glory when it comes like a flood.

The following are some additional guidelines I have used in order to fully enter into creative glory.

CREATE WHAT YOU LIKE AND NEED

When you create, if you make something that you would desire for yourself, there is a good chance that others will desire it too. For example, whenever I pray about the next book I'm going to write, I always find myself being spiritually directed toward writing a book that I myself would like to have on hand at that moment. When I wrote my best-selling book *Moving in Glory Realms*, it was because many people were telling me that they felt "stuck," somehow sensing an invisible ceiling that seemed to be restricting their spiritual growth. I wanted to be able to reach out and hand these people a book containing useful answers to help solve their problems. Little did I realize that I would be the one to write that book! *Moving in Glory Realms* contains a blueprint for personal revival. Today, that book has been translated into various languages. It has helped to bring great spiritual growth to ministry leaders and laypeople around the world.

A similar need compelled me to write *Seeing Angels*. I had been ministering to a Hollywood celebrity who was experiencing a lot of supernatural phenomena, and, over time, I had written many letters to this person regarding the angelic realm. The celebrity was asking important questions that hadn't been answered in other Christian books on the topic, and I recognized that these questions deserved to be addressed. I quickly realized that those letters I had written were important for more than just one person to read, so that correspondence became the basis for the book. Then, little by little, I continued to search the Scriptures, spend time in prayer, and write from my own personal experiences with angels. The book I ended up writing was something I needed and something that others needed as well.

Someone recently wrote to me, "I wanted to let you know how inspired I have been by your book *Seeing Angels*. It's really made a difference in my life, and I feel like I have now been able to see angels." I have people sending me testimonies like that all the time, and it thrills me to no end. This is the beautiful payoff I receive for the hard work and emotional commitment that is involved in writing each book. Yes, creative expression requires sacrifice on many levels, but the end results are always rewarding.

INCREASE PRODUCTIVITY THROUGH MULTIPLE PROJECTS

I always seem to have several creative projects in the works. At any one time, I may be writing two or three books, working on one or more musical projects, and engaging in some personal artistic undertakings in addition to following my regular ministry schedule. This is just the way I am. I always like to have my hands in many projects. And this approach enables me to always move with the flow of creative glory and never force myself against it.

Whenever I feel inspired to write, I sit down, pick up a pen (or turn on my computer), and begin working from the place I left off the last time. If I feel inspired to paint, I pick up my art tools and begin working away. If I sense a new song coming, I sit down at the keyboard and begin playing the music. I have arranged my life in such a way that I am free to "go with the flow."

You may think, "That's a nice privilege for him to have," but you can do this too. It's not so much about what resources you have; it's more about what space you make for creative glory. You must make room for the glory, and this can be done anywhere. For example, when I'm traveling on an airplane and the inspiration to write comes upon me, I begin taking notes on my phone. It's not the most pleasant way to write, and it's certainly not the most convenient, but it is the most accessible for capturing the inspiration of the moment. And that's what counts.

Some people feel they must finish the project they are currently working on before moving on to the next project. It may depend on the person, but, in some ways, this kind of thinking can keep you limited or boxed into a corner. In my own experience, when I feel boxed in, I feel the least creative. The glory realm is a wide and vast dimension filled with unlimited potential.

Whenever I consider the "spaces" in heaven, I never see them as rooms. I see them more as hallways because each space leads to another. Our journey through one space opens up a greater space for us, and on and on. There is no end to the realms of eternity.

We must recognize that there is more than one thing available for us to discover in God at any given time. If the Spirit is teaching you more about His healing power, make room for it. Take notes, writing down everything that He speaks to your heart.

Or, if the Spirit is revealing visions of the glories of heaven to you, pick up your pencil and begin to sketch what you see or grab hold of your paintbrush and begin to paint it.

You may sense God's love overflowing within you, bubbling up inside as simple lyrics to a new song. Pull out your voice recorder and capture the beautiful melodies as they come. I have hundreds of voice recordings on my phone. Some of them contain full choruses, but most are just a line or two that were given to me in a moment of spontaneity. I have learned never to discard these heaven-sent gifts. Today, with the advanced technology available to us, we're able to digitally file and organize music, photos, videos, and other elements of creativity, and this is a great blessing. We can file our creative projects that are in the process of development and then work on them little by little until we're ready to release them to the world around us.

Working on more than one project at a time not only allows us to be moved by the inspiration of creative glory, but it can also cause us to be much more productive. I've often been asked, "Joshua, how do you write so many books so quickly?" While it may seem like I am writing at an accelerated pace, the truth is that I've been carrying many of these books around in my spirit for years. Some books I complete speedily, but others take more time.

A few weeks ago, I discovered three manuscripts that I had started almost twenty years ago but had forgotten about. This discovery was a pleasant surprise. I believe that when we choose to live for God, there are no wasted moments. You may have been working on some projects for quite some time, but perhaps their completion and release have been saved *"for such a time as this"* (Esther 4:14, various translations). Other endeavors that the Spirit leads you to do will be completed quickly and more succinctly. Again, the key is to move and work with creative glory as the Spirit leads.

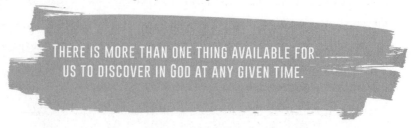

THERE IS MORE THAN ONE THING AVAILABLE FOR US TO DISCOVER IN GOD AT ANY GIVEN TIME.

USE THE POWER OF LIFELINES

I've never met a creative person who likes to be bound by a deadline. In the natural, deadlines feel restrictive and suffocating. However, here is the truth of the matter: unless we set a goal for finalizing a project, it will never be successfully completed. You need goals, and I do too. We all need goals because they push us to finish what we've begun. Maybe, as someone has said, instead of using the term *deadlines*, we should call them *lifelines*. That's really what they are. According to the dictionary, a *lifeline* is "a thing on which someone or something depends or which provides a means of escape from a difficult situation" or "a rope or line used for life-saving, typically one thrown to rescue someone in difficulties in water or one used by sailors to secure themselves to a boat."[41]

In essence, a lifeline helps pull our creative ships into port, where they can be seen. As creative people, we love the adventure of the high seas, exploring new sights, sounds, and experiences. But, at some point, the creative process must come to an end. There should be a point to it all.

As an author, one of the most difficult things for me to do is to finish writing a book. It always seems like there is more that can and should be added. Even after I release my initial manuscript to my publisher, I continue to send my editors rewritten chapters, updated sections, and revisions...until the very last moment when the book goes to the printer. Why? Because there is always more!

This is why we need lifelines. Lifelines are designated dates, times, and occasions when a creative work must be completed in order for us to be able to focus more of our energies on other projects still at hand. As much as I push against them and resist them, I am thankful for the "lifelines" that my publisher sets for me because they enable each book to be finalized and published so that other people can be blessed by my work.

When you set specific goals, you are able to achieve specific success. Allow creative glory to give you lifelines for the projects you currently have in the works. Without lifelines, you may never finish them!

WHEN YOU SET SPECIFIC GOALS,
YOU ARE ABLE TO ACHIEVE SPECIFIC SUCCESS.

---

41. *Lexico*, s.v. "lifeline," https://www.lexico.com/definition/lifeline.

SEASONS OF PREPARATION

There are seasons of spiritual preparation in everyone's life. You may be walking through one right now and feeling pressed up against a wall. But creative release is on the way! The Lord says, "Glory is coming, glory that breaks down barriers and causes doors to open in the Spirit. New portals are opening for you to enter." If you choose to enter them, these portals will open within you as rays of light, going forth to penetrate the hearts and minds of those to whom you are called to minister. In this new glory you're standing in, there are new signs, new wonders, and new miracles. Again, the glory realm is limitless!

You may be facing a transition season. Have faith! Things are about to turn around for the good, as they always do for those who love the Lord. (See Romans 8:28.) Everything you have known in the past will no longer look the same to you in the future. Why? Because there is a more glorious future ahead of you than what you have experienced in the past. You might say, "But the past has been wonderful." Well then, get ready for life to be even *more* wonderful.

For those who feel squeezed and under pressure, remember this: unless the lump of dirty black coal endures the pressure, it never becomes a brilliant, translucent diamond. And that's where you are in this moment. But God is opening a new way for you to live and love. His angels are being released and dispatched to you. Special gifts are being given to you so that you can fulfill everything God has called you to do.

In these difficult days we're living in, don't be sad, and don't be angry. Be glad in the Lord. Be joyful in His glory because what God has ready for you now is greater than what you've known before. Embrace the limitless possibilities in this realm of creative glory.

If you have resisted God in any way in the past, surrender to the Lord right now. Present your struggles and fears to Him. Give Him the areas in which you've been having difficulty. The Bible says that when we come before God's throne of grace, we will find mercy in our time of need. (See Hebrews 4:16.) Give to the Lord the heaviness, the weight, and the oppression you feel. Give it all to the Lord right now. Shake it off and leave it with Him.

That sickness? Shake it off. Shake off the worry. Get rid of it right now. The doubt? Let it go. You are being delivered in the power portals of God's creative glory. You are being set free, and *"if the Son sets you free, you are truly free"* (John 8:36 NLT).

RELEASED IN THE GLORY

I see in the Spirit that the enemy is trying to muzzle you. The enemy wants to silence your praise and shut you down. But the Lord says, "You are free. Nothing will muzzle your praise, your testimony, or the Word of the Lord on your lips." From those lips, God has ordained praise. Your lips were made for praising Him. They were created to exalt Him. I see golden notes coming out of your mouth as part of a new praise that's coming, a brand-new sound that can't be stopped.

You are the shofar of the Lord. He says, "Sound the trumpet on My holy mountain." (See Joel 2:1.) Your sound of praise is shifting the spiritual atmosphere right now, prompting a new beginning, a whole new era. Let the high praises of God be in your mouth and the double-edged sword of the Word be in your hands.

Let's pray together:

Father, in the name of Jesus, we thank You for what You are doing in us. We thank You for the changes You're bringing, the movement of Your Spirit, the impartation of Your gifts that are even now being assigned to us, and the opening and enlargement of spiritual portals over us. Lord, we give ourselves to You completely, not holding anything back. In the mighty name of Jesus, amen!

CREATIVE GLORY! LET THIS GLORY ARISE IN ME!

CONCLUSION: CREATIVE IMPARTATION

In this moment of creative glory, God is realigning, refocusing, resetting, and repositioning you so that you might walk in His ways. A shift is taking place in the atmosphere. You are in a new place in the Spirit. This is a different place, a higher level than you have been in before.

Every word that God has given you is *yes* and *amen*. (See 2 Corinthians 1:20.) Every word that He has given you is true. God doesn't lie, and He watches over His Word to perform it, making it come to pass in your life. (See Numbers 23:19.) His Word will not return to Him void but will go forth and accomplish what it was sent to do. (See Isaiah 55:11.) You are being reconnected to the reality, truth, power, and glory of the Word, and you will go forth in glory!

In the Spirit, right now, I see golden keys being placed into eager and open hands. These keys unlock doors to the miracle realm and the solutions to the problems you face.

I see the Spirit dropping codes into your spirit, and I feel prophetically that these represent the combinations to a safe, a treasury in heaven of the abundant provisions God is giving you access to.

I see God giving you golden shoes, and when they are placed upon your feet, you will be given access to walk in new territories of the Spirit. Thank You, Lord.

Because the glory realm is without limits, you will receive new visions to see into the heavenlies. God wants to show you heavenly plans and heavenly resources of which you will become a conduit. Grab hold of these visions and pull each one down into the earthly realm for manifestation.

> GOD IS REALIGNING, REFOCUSING, RESETTING, AND REPOSITIONING YOU SO THAT YOU MIGHT WALK IN HIS WAYS.

I see a golden quill being placed in your hand. You are being called to write, to transcribe the messages of heaven, the messages of the Lord. You will write in a new way that comes directly from the Spirit to you. Heavenly messages will be given to you that will be published and released in new ways.

I see the Lord giving you golden fruit, fruit of the Spirit that you will manifest in a whole new way. You will learn how to walk in the Spirit, digesting the fruit of the Spirit as never before.

I see a golden mantle being placed upon you. It is not like a coat but more like a robe. It is being placed upon your shoulders and wrapped around you. It is long and drapes all the way down to the floor, covering you. It is the covering of the Lord. This new glory mantle is coming upon you to enable you to walk into what the Lord has called you to do.

The Lord says, "The enemy has tried to bring opposition and distractions, but My Spirit of glory is upon you even now, and what I have called you for, anointed you for, and appointed you for, you will walk in during the days ahead. There is a new realm without limits, a new realm of heavenly authority, and a new glory that I have placed upon you. Receive it and walk in it."

I see creative glory swirling around, and the Lord says, "All you have to do is connect with what I'm doing and you will manifest the fruit of it. Creative glory is your portion, so walk in it."

There is a fresh anointing on you, a greater glory for the ministry God has called you to fulfill. His glory will be released from you like rays of light, emanating from the very core of your being, where He lives.

God is opening new doors of opportunity for you. Embrace them without fear. Walk into these opportunities. Jump into these opportunities. Soar into these opportunities! Each one represents a new place of creative glory in your life.

There are new businesses, ministries, careers, relationships, and so many other ideas in this creative-glory realm. God doesn't want anyone to fail or be destroyed financially, spiritually, or emotionally. His desire is to build you up and increase you in every aspect of your life. His plan is to bless you so that you can be a blessing to many others. Let creative glory rise within you!

WE ARE THE MUSIC MAKERS

I want to close this book with a portion of an often-cited poem written by Arthur O'Shaughnessy in 1873. It captures the heart and soul of creatives, and it is my prayer that it will become an encouragement to you as you move forward in these realms of *Creative Glory*.

We are the music makers,
    And we are the dreamers of dreams,
Wandering by lone sea-breakers,—
    And sitting by desolate streams;
World-losers and world-forsakers,
    On whom the pale moon gleams:
Yet we are the movers and shakers
    Of the world for ever, it seems.

With wonderful deathless ditties
We build up the world's great cities,
    And out of a fabulous story
    We fashion an empire's glory:
One man with a dream, at pleasure,
    Shall go forth and conquer a crown;
And three with a new song's measure
Can trample a kingdom down.

We, in the ages lying
    In the buried past of the earth,
Built Nineveh with our sighing,
    And Babel itself with our mirth;
And o'erthrew them with prophesying
    To the old of the new world's worth;
For each age is a dream that is dying,
    Or one that is coming to birth.[42]

---

42. Arthur O'Shaughnessy, "Ode," Poetry Foundation, https://www.poetryfoundation.org/poems/54933/ode-.

Photography by Dustin Mitchell @creativedust

ABOUT THE AUTHOR

*J*oshua Mills is an internationally recognized, ordained minister of the gospel, as well as a recording artist and keynote conference speaker. He is also the author of more than twenty books and training manuals. His other books with Whitaker House include *7 Divine Mysteries*, *Power Portals*, *Moving in Glory Realms*, and *Seeing Angels*, all with corresponding study guides and audiobooks, and *Angelic Activations*.

Joshua is well known for the supernatural atmosphere that he carries and for his unique insights into the glory realm and prophetic sound. Wherever Joshua ministers, the Word of God is confirmed by miraculous signs and wonders that testify of Jesus Christ. He is regarded as a spiritual forerunner in the body of Christ. For many years, he has helped people discover the life-shifting truths of salvation, healing, and deliverance for spirit, soul, and body.

Joshua and his wife, Janet, cofounded International Glory Ministries and have ministered in over seventy-five nations on six continents. Featured together in several film documentaries and print articles, they have ministered to millions around the world through radio, television, and their weekly webcast, *Glory Bible Study*. They enjoy life with their three children, Lincoln, Liberty, and Legacy, and their puppy, Buttercup.

www.joshuamills.com

Welcome to Our House!

We Have a Special Gift for You

It is our privilege and pleasure to share in your love of Christian books. We are committed to bringing you authors and books that feed, challenge, and enrich your faith.

To show our appreciation, we invite you to sign up to receive a specially selected **Reader Appreciation Gift**, with our compliments. Just go to the Web address at the bottom of this page.

God bless you as you seek a deeper walk with Him!

WE HAVE A GIFT FOR YOU. VISIT:

whpub.me/nonfictionthx

WHITAKER
HOUSE